POLICING
THE POLICE

Other Books in the At Issue Series:

POLICING THE POLICE

David Bender, *Publisher*
Bruno Leone, *Executive Editor*

Katie de Koster, *Managing Editor*
Scott Barbour, *Series Editor*

Paul A. Winters, *Book Editor*

An Opposing Viewpoints Series®

Greenhaven Press, Inc.
San Diego, California

Library of Congress Cataloging-in-Publication Data

At issue: policing the police / book editor, Paul A. Winters.
        p.   cm. — (At issue series) (An opposing viewpoints series)
    Includes bibliographical references and index.
    ISBN 1-56510-262-2 (pbk.) — ISBN 1-56510-295-9 (lib.).
    1. Public relations—Police—United States. 2. Police—United
States—Complaints against. 3. Police administration—United States.
4. Police corruption—United States. I. Winters, Paul A., 1965-   .
II. Title: Policing the police. III. Series. IV. Series: Opposing viewpoints
series (Unnumbered)
HV7936.P8A85   1995   94-28348
363.2′0973—dc20   CIP
                                                                AC

© 1995 by Greenhaven Press, Inc., PO Box 289009,
San Diego, CA 92198-9009

Printed in the U.S.A.

Table of Contents

Introduction

The videotaped beating of Rodney King in Los Angeles on March 3, 1991, was a watershed event. With the media's spotlight on the case, Americans were forced to confront the issue of police use of force. A scandal emerging the following year in New York City demonstrated a different danger. The arrest of six police officers on drug charges in May 1992 resulted in the exposure of widespread corruption and abuse of power within the New York Police Department (NYPD). The commissions impaneled to investigate both incidents found a police culture that fostered brutality and corruption—but came to different conclusions about the causes of and remedies for that culture.

Brutality in Los Angeles

The events surrounding the arrest and beating of Rodney King were widely publicized. In the early hours of March 3, 1991, Los Angeles police and California Highway Patrol officers pursued and eventually stopped Rodney King's speeding car. A bystander videotaped part of what followed: the police delivered approximately fifty blows to King with their batons. After the videotape was shown on television worldwide, four Los Angeles Police Department (LAPD) officers—Sergeant Stacey Koon and Officers Lawrence Powell, Timothy Wind, and Theodore Briseno—were tried in a California state court on charges of excessive use of force.

According to Koon, in his book *Presumed Guilty: The Tragedy of the Rodney King Affair*, the criminal defense of the police officers rested on their belief that they were doing their job as their training and as LAPD guidelines prescribed. It also rested on the portrayal of King as "a really monster guy, a felony evader seen committing numerous serious traffic violations . . . a PCP-dusted felony suspect." Although the jury apparently accepted this defense, acquitting the officers of the charges, announcement of the verdict on April 29, 1992, sparked a weekend-long riot in Los Angeles and violent demonstrations in other cities. The four LAPD officers were later tried in a federal court on charges of violating Rodney King's civil rights. Two of the officers—Sergeant Koon and Officer Powell—were found guilty and received prison sentences.

Corruption in New York City

National attention has also been given to a case in New York City. In May 1992, six NYPD officers were arrested in Suffolk County, New York, on charges of drug trafficking. The subsequent investigation revealed that the officers were sharing among themselves about $8,000 a week in profits from various illegal activities that ranged from taking bribes to protect certain drug dealers to selling drugs seized in criminal investigations. Remarked Michael Armstrong, who had investigated previous cases of corruption in the NYPD, "It seems cops have gone into competition with

7

street criminals." Convicted officers admitted that they would use their radios to organize raids against rival drug dealers, in which they would beat people and steal money, drugs, and guns; they would later sell the drugs and guns for profit.

The investigation also revealed that several complaints against the officers had been received but never followed up by the NYPD's anti-corruption unit. These officers testified that they never feared detection due to the "blue wall of silence"—the unwritten law that police officers do not inform on other police officers. Even when other officers were willing to come forward with information about corruption, it was often ignored by superiors. Inquiries by the Internal Affairs Division (IAD), responsible for anti-corruption efforts in the NYPD, were often mishandled or dropped for a declared "lack of evidence," according to investigators looking into this case.

The commissions examine police culture

In late March 1991, then-mayor of Los Angeles Tom Bradley formed the Independent Commission on the Los Angeles Police Department as a response to charges that the Rodney King beating was merely one instance of a widespread problem of police brutality. The commission, chaired by lawyer William Christopher and consequently known as the Christopher Commission, held public hearings in Los Angeles. It came to the conclusion that the LAPD leadership in general and Chief Daryl Gates in particular were responsible for a culture within the LAPD that tolerated, and thereby promoted, brutality. The commission reported that while only a few officers were responsible for the majority of cases of brutality, failure by superiors to discipline these few officers created the impression that brutality was condoned.

The commission also concluded that the LAPD's style of policing fostered brutality. The LAPD pioneered the use of radio-dispatched patrol cars, allowing officers to patrol a beat in cars rather than on foot. Officers respond to crimes only when they are called—usually on a 911 system— or when they witness criminal activity. The Christopher Commission concluded that this style of policing creates a siege mentality that alienates police officers from the community and that this alienation leads to unnecessarily aggressive confrontations and to brutality.

On the other side of the country, the Mollen Commission, named for its chairman, former New York judge Milton Mollen, was formed in July 1992. The commission revived the work of the 1970–72 Knapp Commission, which had investigated the NYPD's failure to prosecute corruption uncovered in 1968 by NYPD officer Frank Serpico. The Mollen Commission charged that the remedies put in place by the Knapp Commission— such as establishing the NYPD Internal Affairs Division—had been neglected, allowing corruption to return in a worse form than before, with officers now actively engaged in criminal activity. The Mollen Commission found that the NYPD leadership feared a scandal so much that they preferred the quiet continuation of corruption to its public revelation.

It was also suggested by such observers as Richard Lacayo of *Time* magazine that the NYPD's style of community policing provided police with opportunities for corrupt activity. "Getting to know the neighborhood can mean finding more occasions for bribe taking," according to Lacayo. He argued that the tremendous amounts of money circulating in the drug trade were a tempting incentive to illegal activity, and that the lack of supervision of police on foot patrols allowed corruption to go undetected by the NYPD leadership. Additional arrests in New York City in April 1994 seemed to suggest that police corruption is a widespread problem, particularly in poorer, more crime-ridden neighborhoods of New York, such as Harlem and parts of the Bronx.

The recommendations of the commissions

Both the Christopher and Mollen Commissions concluded that an "us-versus-them" culture among police led to the problems of brutality and corruption. The Christopher Commission recommended community policing as a way to change that culture. It was the commission's opinion that community policing would provide police officers the opportunity to become acquainted with the people they serve, instead of just with the criminals they arrest. "Community policing concepts, if successfully implemented, offer the prospect of effective crime prevention and substantially improved community relations," in the words of the Christopher Commission report. The Mollen Commission in New York, where community policing has been in place and, some say, has provided opportunities for corruption, recommends civilian oversight to change police culture. In the Mollen Commission's assessment, a civilian monitor would "ensure that the [NYPD] makes effective efforts to reform the conditions and attitudes that nurture and perpetuate corruption and brutality."

A historical overview of police reform begins this book, along with the recommendations of the Christopher and Mollen Commissions. *At Issue: Policing the Police* examines the views of those who say that society should support and understand the police and allow them to do the job assigned to them—to catch criminals. Also explored are several recommendations for police reform, from civilian oversight to further professionalization.

The incident that prompted the formation of the Christopher Commission—the beating of Rodney King—was a watershed because it forced Americans to examine relations between their communities and the police they hire to serve them. *Rolling Stone* reporter Jon Katz writes that at the heart of the issue "lie questions about the most fundamental concepts and traditions of policing: who and what the police ought to be." This anthology examines these traditions and concepts as well as proposals for changing them.

1

The History of Police Reform: An Overview

Richard L. Worsnop

Richard L. Worsnop is associate editor of the CQ Researcher, *a weekly research report on public policy issues.*

Although touted as the latest trend in police reforms, community policing is in fact a return to early policing principles imported from 19th-century England that stressed close ties between police officers and the communities they serve. Because of its lack of centralized control, this form of policing fostered corruption in America's early police departments, particularly during the Prohibition era when opportunities for bribe taking and interference by criminals were widespread. Police reforms from the 1930s to the 1950s sought to establish "professionalism" among police forces by introducing military-like command structures and higher performance standards. Combined with the introduction of advanced communication technology and patrol cars, requiring fewer police to patrol larger areas, professional policing distanced police from communities according to critics. These critics see the March 1991 beating of Rodney King by officers of the Los Angeles Police Department (which pioneered professional policing) as the inevitable result of these reforms. They call for a return to principles of community policing to restore ties between the police and the community.

Though community policing is often touted as the latest wrinkle in law enforcement, its supporters acknowledge that it isn't new at all. In fact, they say, community policing is basically an updated version of the principles laid down more than 160 years ago by Sir Robert Peel, the British statesman.

19th-century roots

While serving as home secretary in the Duke of Wellington's Cabinet in 1829, Peel persuaded Parliament to approve the Metropolitan Police Act. The law established the first police force with law-enforcement authority over all of London.

Richard L. Worsnop, "Community Policing," CQ *Researcher*, February 5, 1993. Reprinted with permission.

Opponents voiced concern that the force could facilitate the rise of tyranny, but Peel allayed their fears by stressing the officers' close ties to the community. "The police are the public," he declared, "and the public are the police." The Peel philosophy of law enforcement was emphatically proactive, making crime prevention the top priority.

Peel was no innovator, for many of his ideas on law enforcement were drawn from centuries of English tradition. "In the Anglo-Saxon England of a thousand years ago," political scientist Louis A. Radelet wrote in *The Police and the Community*, "every able-bodied freeman was a police officer. Every male from 15 to 60 maintained such arms as he could afford. When the hue and cry was raised, every man within earshot dropped whatever he was doing and joined in the pursuit of the transgressor. Not to do so was serious neglect of duty."[1]

The Peel model of policing was adopted in 1844 by New York, the first American city to establish a police force, and then by many other communities across the country. Citizen involvement in policing was especially noticeable in the frontier West, where vigilante activity was commonplace.

"Yet the system of political control of the police that developed in America differed from the English model," Radelet noted. "The decentralized pattern of early American police tended to place considerable power in the hands of ward and precinct politicians." This arrangement, events were to show, "became a plus-and-minus element in police–community relations."[2]

Police corruption

The biggest minus undoubtedly was corruption of the law-enforcement process. Whether it took the form of citizen bribes or criminal interference, corruption surfaced early as a recurrent problem. For instance, it was relatively easy to "buy" the sheriff in many Western towns in the latter half of the 19th century.

The extent of police corruption at the turn of the 20th century was laid bare by the noted muckraking journalist Lincoln Steffens in *The Shame of the Cities*, a collection of articles written for *McClure's* magazine.

One piece, focusing entirely on police scandals in Minneapolis, created a nationwide uproar. With the full cooperation of the mayor and the police force, Steffens disclosed, criminals virtually took over the city until a 1902 grand jury investigation caused the conspiracy to collapse.

Police reform movement

Though the Minneapolis scandal was hardly unique at the time, the forces of police reform were slow to respond. It was only with the advent of Prohibition in the 1920s, and the vastly greater opportunities for official corruption that accompanied it, that a reform movement championed the "professional" approach to law enforcement that remains the standard in most cities today. In [Temple University professor of criminal justice] James J. Fyfe's opinion, the reforms "were largely modeled after J. Edgar Hoover's FBI, which dictated that police should be a thin blue line, isolated from the community, because you can't trust the community."

A prime objective of the reformers was severing the police-politician tie, regarded as a leading source of urban crime. The city charter adopted by Los Angeles in 1925 was hailed as a milestone in this regard. The charter placed the police department under the control of a five-member board of police commissioners appointed by the mayor. The commission had the power to name, discipline and remove the police chief.

The reform movement made headway elsewhere, too. One goal was to make police officers measure up to professional standards. Until about 1930, amateurism and incompetence held sway. Most officers lacked even a high school education, received little training, earned low pay and remained on the force well beyond normal retirement age.

[O.W.] Wilson advocated a clear-cut chain of command along military lines, specialization of tasks, delegation of authority and responsibility and close supervision of officers on patrol duty.

The most widely copied formula for police professionalism was the model used by Orlando W. Wilson when he was police chief of Wichita, Kansas, from 1928 to 1939. Wilson advocated a clear-cut chain of command along military lines, specialization of tasks, delegation of authority and responsibility and close supervision of officers on patrol duty. He also stressed the importance of higher education and personal integrity for police officers.

Law enforcement agencies nationwide remade themselves in the Wilsonian image in the 1930s, '40s and '50s, a period when crime rates were relatively low.

For the most part, police reform achieved its objectives. Professor George L. Kelling of Northeastern University's Department of Criminal Justice noted that "crime and arrest statistics became enshrined as the measures of police performance; police professionalism came to be identified with educated chiefs of police and centralized command and control; linkages with neighborhoods and communities were severed and what was identified as police *officer* professionalism—remoteness and distance from citizens—came to be seen as the norm of professional police service."[3] And corruption virtually ceased.

Off the streets, into patrol cars

As these changes were taking place, police forces came to rely increasingly on motor vehicles and advanced communications technology. "What largely began as a move to separate police from citizens and improve control over line officers—putting police in radio patrol cars—was rationalized into preventive control and rapid response to calls for service," observed Kelling.[4]

Another reason for the change was budgetary—fewer officers could cover more territory in a motor vehicle. Today, with the 911 system for emergency calls in operation almost everywhere, big-city police spend much of their time rushing from one crime scene to another.

The Los Angeles Police Department (LAPD) led the way in embracing the vehicle-based, reactive approach to law enforcement. Among other innovations, the LAPD pioneered the use of paramilitary Special Weapons and Tactics (SWAT) teams, helicopters and motorized battering rams. The department's wide array of vehicles and support equipment enabled it to respond to reported crimes rapidly and in impressive force. More important, the technological muscle helped offset a chronic shortage of patrol officers.

Efficiency and shorter response time were not achieved without cost, however. Community residents came to look upon police as alien figures who rarely showed up except after a crime was committed.

"Over the past 40 years or so," says Fyfe, "we have defined the professional policeman in a very cold, distant kind of manner—a Joe Friday, steely-eyed, civil to everybody but not very friendly kind of officer. We've moved away from the first principle of policing, which is that a police force should be accountable and responsive to the community."

Impact of the Rodney King beating in L.A.

For many law-enforcement experts, the beating of Rodney G. King by a group of Los Angeles police officers in March 1991 exposed the shortcomings of professional policing. King, a 25-year-old black man, was beaten and kicked by four LAPD officers after a high-speed auto chase. He also was struck twice by a Taser electric stun gun.

All the while, without the knowledge of anyone involved in the incident, a plumbing store manager named George Holliday was recording the scene from his apartment balcony with a video camera. When the two-minute tape was broadcast over the Cable News Network (CNN) two days later, King became an instant symbol of police brutality.

Commenting on the case, Herman Goldstein said: "it's inconceivable that a police officer imbued with community policing would engage in that type of behavior."[5]

For many law-enforcement experts, the beating of Rodney G. King by a group of Los Angeles police officers in March 1991 exposed the shortcomings of professional policing.

The commission appointed to investigate the LAPD after the King beating seemed to agree. "LAPD officers are encouraged to command and to confront, not to communicate," the panel stated. "Community policing concepts, if successfully implemented, offer the prospect of effective crime prevention and substantially improved community relations." The department, it added, "must gain an adequate understanding of what is important to particularly communities."[6]

New approach to policing

Even before the Los Angeles commission issued its report, professional policing methods were beginning to lose favor in law-enforcement circles. In 1967, the President's Commission on Law Enforcement and Administration of Justice stated: "Improving community relations involves not only instituting programs and changing procedures and practices, but re-examining fundamental attitudes. The police will have to learn to listen patiently and understandingly to people who are openly critical of them or hostile to them, since those people are precisely the ones with whom relations need to be improved. . . . [P]olice–citizen relationships on the street [must] become person-to-person encounters rather than the black-versus-white, oppressed-versus-oppressor confrontations they too often are."[7]

In another rebuke to conventional wisdom, a 1974 study conducted for the Police Foundation cast doubt on the effectiveness of one of professional policing's basic tactics: routine patrol in marked police cruisers. During a year-long experiment in Kansas City, Missouri, researchers found no significant difference in crime levels when patrol levels were cut to less than 40 percent of normal or increased to more than 200 percent of normal.[8]

Meanwhile, foundations were being laid for a new philosophy of law enforcement that would address the failures of professional policing and return to the principles enunciated by Robert Peel. The tenets of this approach emerged piecemeal after considerable debate and many studies. Goldstein cites the following six points as guiding principles of the new "common wisdom":

- The police do much more than deal with crime; they deal with many forms of behavior that are not defined as criminal.
- The wide range of functions that police are expected to perform, including dealing with fear and enforcing public order, are appropriate functions for the police; from the perspective of the community, they may be as important as the tasks the police perform in dealing with behavior labeled criminal.
- Too much dependence in the past has been placed on the criminal law in order to get the police job done; arrest and prosecution are simply not an effective way to handle much of what constitutes police business. And even if potentially effective, it may not be possible to use the criminal justice system in some jurisdictions because it is so overloaded.
- Police use a wide range of methods—formal and informal—in getting their job done. "Law enforcement" is only one method among many.
- Police, of necessity, must exercise broad discretion, including deciding whether to arrest in situations in which there is ample evidence that a criminal law has been violated.
- The police are not autonomous; the sensitive function they perform in our society requires that they be accountable, through the political process, to the community.[9]

To make community policing work, forging strong personal ties between police officers and neighborhood residents is crucial. The reason is that police need a constant flow of information to prevent and control crime. Crime can flourish when such information is lacking, according to [the late] Robert C. Trojanowicz, [former] director of the National Center for Community Policing at Michigan State University, because "the probability of solving crimes and apprehending offenders is exceedingly low without the assistance and cooperation of neighborhood residents."[10]

Community policing's champion: Lee Brown

Of the nation's current or former law-enforcement executives, Lee P. Brown is the best-known advocate of community policing. He championed the concept during his eight years as Houston's police chief (1982–1990) and his two and a half years as police commissioner in New York City (January 1990–August 1992).

To improve police–community relations, he urged that beats be drawn to "coincide with natural neighborhood boundaries, rather than in an arbitrary fashion that meets the needs of the police department." He also made sure that beat and shift assignments were made on a permanent (as opposed to rotating) basis so that beat officers could become "an integral part of the community."[11]

[P]olice–citizen relationships on the street [must] become person-to-person encounters rather than the black-versus-white, oppressed-versus-oppressor confrontations they too often are.

These steps embodied Brown's conviction that community policing makes the beat officer "the most important person in the neighborhood." As New York police commissioner, he regarded the cop on the beat "as a manager, not just answering calls, not just walking the beat, but being able to do problem analysis, knowing the people, being accessible." He also sought to "enhance the patrol officer's status to make it equal to any other in the department" and to open up "a career path in patrol so that people can spend whole careers in patrol."[12]

As Brown sees it, one of the chief goals of community policing is to "end the cycle of responding to the same locations to handle the same or similar complaints." A more fruitful approach, he feels, is to find and try to eliminate the underlying problem that produces repeated complaints, often through the 911 emergency phone line. Attacking the root causes of crime can make law enforcement more cost-effective he says.

Brown adds that community police officers must be prepared to deal also with "quality of life" issues like rowdy teenagers, loud noises late at night and abandoned autos and houses. These often are of more immediate concern to neighborhood residents than major crime,[13] and not without reason. Experience shows that a deteriorating neighborhood lowers citizen morale and fosters an atmosphere in which crime can thrive.

Police cannot be expected to solve quality-of-life complaints by themselves, Brown feels. Instead, they should try to organize residents or enlist the services of a government agency to tackle such problems. "That doesn't mean that police officers become social workers," he says. "It does mean that police officers need to deal with solving problems."[14]

Notes

1. Louis A. Radelet, *The Police and the Community* (fourth edition). Macmillan Publishing Co., 1986, p. 5.

2. *Ibid.*, p. 6.

3. George L. Kelling, "The Community Paradigm of Policing," in Radelet, *op. cit.*, p. 57.

4. *Ibid.*

5. *Quoted in Time*, April 1, 1991, p. 22. For background, see "Police Brutality," *The CQ Researcher*, Sept. 6, 1991, pp. 633-656.

6. *Report of the Independent Commission on the Los Angeles Police Department*, July 9, 1991. The commission was headed by former Deputy Secretary of

State Warren M. Christopher, who has since been appointed as Secretary of State by President Clinton.

7. President's Commission on Law Enforcement and Administration of Justice, *The Challenge of Crime in a Free Society*, 1967, p. 100.

8. George L. Kelling, *et al.*, *The Kansas City Preventive Patrol Experiment: A Technical Report*, 1974.

9. Herman Goldstein, *Problem-Oriented Policing*, McGraw-Hill Publishing Co., 1990, p. 11.

10. Robert C. Trojanowicz, "Foot Patrol: Improving Police-Citizen Contact," in Radelet, *op. cit.*, p. 481.

11. Lee P. Brown, "Community Policing: A Practical Guide for Police Officials," *The Police Chief*, August 1989, p. 76.

12. Alan M. Webber, "Crime and Management: An Interview With New York City Police Commissioner Lee P. Brown," *Harvard Business Review*, May–June 1991, p. 125.

13. A community policing survey conducted in Portland, Ore., in 1989 found that the 12 most frequently cited neighborhood problems were abandoned buildings, burglary, car prowls, chronic theft/vandalism, drugs, gangs, loitering youths, parks, problem liquor outlets, prostitution, street people and traffic.

14. Webber, *op. cit.*, p. 126.

2
Brutality in the Los Angeles Police Department

Independent Commission on the Los Angeles Police Department

The Independent Commission on the Los Angeles Police Department, chaired by William Christopher, was formed in March 1991 by then-Mayor of Los Angeles Tom Bradley following the videotaped beating of Rodney G. King.

Empanelled to investigate the structural causes of police brutality by the LAPD, the Independent Commission on the Los Angeles Police Department (or Christopher Commission as it was popularly known) released its report in July 1991, four months after the Rodney King beating incident. The Commission found within the LAPD a police "culture" that promoted racism; recruitment and training practices that perpetuated this culture; a complaint procedure that discouraged citizen complaints; a failure to discipline officers who repeatedly used excessive force; and a lack of leadership in dealing with discipline issues. An "us-versus-them" mentality among officers was blamed in part on the patrol style of the LAPD, where officers patrol in radio-equipped cars instead of on foot. The recommendations of the Commission include a call for community policing as a way to change the police "culture," a change in training practices, and reform of the disciplinary system.

The videotaped beating of Rodney G. King by three uniformed officers of the Los Angeles Police Department, in the presence of a sergeant and with a large group of other officers standing by, galvanized public demand for evaluation and reform of police procedures involving the use of force. In the wake of the incident and the resulting widespread outcry, the Independent Commission on the Los Angeles Police Department was created. The Commission sought to examine all aspects of the law enforcement structure in Los Angeles that might cause or contribute to the problem of excessive force. The Report is unanimous.

The King beating raised fundamental questions about the LAPD, including:

- the apparent failure to control or discipline officers with repeated

Summary (pp. 1-14), *Report of the Independent Commission on the Los Angeles Police Department,* July 9, 1991. Reprinted with permission.

complaints of excessive force;
- concerns about the LAPD's "culture" and officers' attitudes toward racial and other minorities;
- the difficulties the public encounters in attempting to make complaints against LAPD officers;
- the role of the LAPD leadership and civilian oversight authorities in addressing or contributing to these problems.

These and related questions and concerns form the basis for the Commission's work.

Los Angeles and its police force

The LAPD is headed by Police Chief Daryl Gates with an executive staff currently consisting of 2 assistant chiefs, 5 deputy chiefs, and 17 commanders. The City Charter provides that the Department is ultimately under the control and oversight of the five-member civilian Board of Police Commissioners. The Office of Operations, headed by Assistant Chief Robert Vernon, accounts for approximately 84% of the Department's personnel, including most patrol officers and detectives. The Office of Operations has 18 separate geographic areas within the City, divided among 4 bureaus (Central, South, West, and Valley). There are currently about 8,450 sworn police officers, augmented by more than 2,000 civilian LAPD employees.

While the overall rate of violent crime in the United States increased three and one-half times between 1960 and 1989, the rate in Los Angeles during the same period was more than twice the national average. According to 1986 data recently published by the Police Foundation, the Los Angeles police were the busiest among the officers in the nation's largest six cities. As crime rates soar, police officers must contend with more and more potential and actual violence each day. One moment officers must confront a life-threatening situation; the next they must deal with citizen problems requiring understanding and kindness. The difficulties of policing in Los Angeles are compounded by its vast geographic area and the ethnic diversity of its population. The 1990 census data reflect how enormous that diversity is: Latinos constitute 40% of the total population; Whites 37%; African-Americans 13%; and Asian/Pacific Islanders and others 10%. Of the police departments of the six largest United States cities, the LAPD has the fewest officers per resident and the fewest officers per square mile. Yet the LAPD boasts more arrests per officer than other forces. Moreover, by all accounts, the LAPD is generally efficient, sophisticated, and free of corruption.

The problem of excessive force

LAPD officers exercising physical force must comply with the Department's Use of Force Policy and Guidelines, as well as California law. Both the LAPD Policy and the Penal Code require that force be reasonable; the Policy also requires that force be necessary. An officer may resort to force only where he or she faces a credible threat, and then may use only the minimum amount necessary to control the suspect.

The Commission has found that there are a significant number of LAPD officers who repetitively misuse force and persistently ignore the written policies and guidelines of the Department regarding force. The evidence obtained by the Commission shows that this group has received inadequate supervisory and management attention.

Former Assistant Chief Jesse Brewer testified that this lack of management attention and accountability is the "essence of the excessive force problem. . . . We know who the bad guys are. Reputations become well known, especially to the sergeants and then of course to lieutenants and the captains in the areas. . . . But I don't see anyone bring these people up. . . ." Assistant Chief David Dotson testified that "we have failed miserably" to hold supervisors accountable for excessive force by officers under their command. Interviews with a large number of present and former LAPD officers yield similar conclusions. Senior and rank-and-file officers generally stated that a significant number of officers tended to use force excessively, that these problem officers were well known in their divisions, that the Department's efforts to control or discipline those officers were inadequate, and that their supervisors were not held accountable for excessive use of force by officers in their command.

A significant group of problem officers poses a much higher risk of excessive force than other officers.

The Commission's extensive computerized analysis of the data provided by the Department (personnel complaints, use of force reports, and reports of officer-involved shootings) shows that a significant group of problem officers poses a much higher risk of excessive force than other officers:

- Of approximately 1,800 officers against whom an allegation of excessive force or improper tactics was made from 1986 to 1990, more than 1,400 had only 1 or 2 allegations. But 183 officers had 4 or more allegations, 44 had 6 or more, 16 had 8 or more, and one had 16 such allegations.
- Of nearly 6,000 officers identified as involved in use of force reports from January 1987 to March 1991, more than 4,000 had fewer than 5 reports each. But 63 officers had 20 or more reports each. The top 5% of the officers (ranked by number of reports) accounted for more than 20% of all reports. . . .

Blending the data disclosed even more troubling patterns. For example, in the years covered, one officer had 13 allegations of excessive force and improper tactics, 5 other complaint allegations, 28 use of force reports, and 1 shooting. Another had 6 excessive force/improper tactics allegations, 19 other complaint allegations, 10 use of force reports, and 3 shootings. A third officer had 7 excessive force/improper tactics allegations, 7 other complaint allegations, 27 use of force reports, and 1 shooting.

A review of personnel files of the 44 officers identified from the LAPD database who had 6 or more allegations of excessive force or improper tactics for the period 1986 through 1990 disclosed that the picture conveyed was often incomplete and at odds with contemporaneous comments appearing in complaint files. As a general matter, the performance evaluation reports for those problem officers were very positive, documenting every complimentary comment received and expressing optimism about the officer's progress in the Department. The performance evaluations generally did not give an accurate picture of the officer's disciplinary history, failing to record "sustained" complaints or to discuss their significance, and failing to assess the officer's judgment and contacts with the public in light of disturbing patterns of complaints.

The existence of a significant number of officers with an unacceptable and improper attitude regarding the use of force is supported by the Commission's extensive review of computer messages sent to and from patrol cars throughout the City over the units' Mobile Digital Terminals (MDTs). The Commission's staff examined 182 days of MDT transmissions selected from the period from November 1989 to March 1991. Although the vast majority of messages reviewed consisted of routine police communications, there were hundreds of improper messages, including scores in which officers talked about beating suspects: "Capture him, beat him and treat him like dirt. . . ." Officers also used the communications system to express their eagerness to be involved in shooting incidents. The transmissions also make clear that some officers enjoy the excitement of a pursuit and view it as an opportunity for violence against a fleeing suspect.

The patrol car transmissions can be monitored by a field supervisor and are stored in a database where they could be (but were not) audited. That many officers would feel free to type messages about force under such circumstances suggests a serious problem with respect to excessive force. That supervisors made no effort to monitor or control those messages evidences a significant breakdown in the Department's management responsibility.

The Commission also reviewed the LAPD's investigation and discipline of the officers involved in all 83 civil lawsuits alleging excessive or improper force by LAPD officers for the period 1986 through 1990 that resulted in a settlement or judgment of more than $15,000. A majority of cases involved clear and often egregious officer misconduct resulting in serious injury or death to the victim. The LAPD's investigation of these 83 cases was deficient in many respects, and discipline against the officers involved was frequently light and often nonexistent.

While the precise size and identity of the problem group of officers cannot be specified without significant further investigation, its existence must be recognized and addressed. The LAPD has a number of tools to promote and enforce its policy that only reasonable and necessary force be used by officers. There are rewards and incentives such as promotions and pay upgrades. The discipline system exists to impose sanctions for misconduct. Officers can be reassigned. Supervisors can monitor and counsel officers under their command. Officers can be trained at the Police Academy and, more importantly, in the field, in the proper use of force.

The Commission believes that the Department has not made sufficient efforts to use those tools effectively to address the significant number of officers who appear to be using force excessively and improperly. The leadership of the LAPD must send a much clearer and more effective message that excessive force will not be tolerated and that officers and their supervisors will be evaluated to an important extent by how well they abide by and advance the Department's policy regarding use of force.

Racism and bias

The problem of excessive force is aggravated by racism and bias within the LAPD. That nexus is sharply illustrated by the results of a survey recently taken by the LAPD of the attitudes of its sworn officers. The survey of 960 officers found that approximately one-quarter (24.5%) of 650 officers responding agreed that "racial bias (prejudice) on the part of officers toward minority citizens currently exists and contributes to a negative interaction between police and community." More than one-quarter (27.6%) agreed that "an officer's prejudice towards the suspect's race may lead to the use of excessive force."

The Commission's review of MDT transmissions revealed an appreciable number of disturbing and recurrent racial remarks. Some of the remarks describe minorities through animal analogies ("sounds like monkey-slapping time"). Often made in the context of discussing pursuits or beating suspects, the offensive remarks cover the spectrum of racial and ethnic minorities in the City ("I would love to drive down Slauson with a flame thrower . . . we would have a barbecue"; "I almost got me a Mexican last night but he dropped the dam gun to quick, lots of wit"). The officers typing the MDT messages apparently had little concern that they would be disciplined for making such remarks. Supervisors failed to monitor the messages or to impose discipline for improper remarks and were themselves frequently the source of offensive comments when in the field.

Attitudes of prejudice and intolerance are translated into unacceptable behavior in the field.

These attitudes of prejudice and intolerance are translated into unacceptable behavior in the field. Testimony from a variety of witnesses depicts the LAPD as an organization with practices and procedures that are conducive to discriminatory treatment and officer misconduct directed to members of minority groups. Witnesses repeatedly told of LAPD officers' verbally harassing minorities, detaining African-American and Latino men who fit certain generalized descriptions of suspects, employing unnecessarily invasive or humiliating tactics in minority neighborhoods, and using excessive force. While the Commission does not purport to adjudicate the validity of any one of these numerous complaints, the intensity and frequency of them reveal a serious problem.

Bias within the LAPD is not confined to officers' treatment of the public, but is also reflected in conduct directed to fellow officers who are members of racial or ethnic minority groups. The MDT messages and other evidence suggest that minority officers are still too frequently subjected to racist slurs and comments and to discriminatory treatment within the Department. While the relative number of officers who openly make racially derogatory comments or treat minority officers in a demeaning manner is small, their attitudes and behavior have a large impact because of the failure of supervisors to enforce vigorously and consistently the Department's policies against racism. That failure conveys to minority and non-minority officers alike the message that such conduct is in practice condoned by the Department.

The LAPD has made substantial progress in hiring minorities and women since the 1981 consent decree settling discrimination lawsuits against the Department. That effort should continue, including efforts to recruit Asians and other minorities who are not covered by the consent decree. The Department's statistics show, however, that the vast majority of minority officers are concentrated in the entry-level police officer ranks in the Department. More than 80% of African-American, Latino and Asian officers hold the rank of Police Officer I–III. Many minority officers cite white dominance of managerial positions within the LAPD as one reason for the Department's continued tolerance of racially motivated language and behavior.

LAPD officers are encouraged to command and to confront, not to communicate.

Bias within the LAPD is not limited to racist and ethnic prejudices but includes strongly felt bias based on gender and sexual orientation. Current LAPD policy prohibits all discrimination, including that based on sexual orientation. A tension remains, however, between the LAPD's official policy and actual practice. The Commission believes that the LAPD must act to implement fully its formal policy of nondiscrimination in the recruitment and promotion of gay and lesbian officers.

A 1987 LAPD study concluded that female officers were subjected to a double standard and subtle harassment and were not accepted as part of the working culture. As revealed in interviews of many of the officers charged with training new recruits, the problem has not abated since 1987. Although female LAPD officers are in fact performing effectively, they are having a difficult time being accepted on a full and equal basis.

The Commission heard substantial evidence that female officers utilize a style of policing that minimizes the use of excessive force. Data examined by the Commission indicate that LAPD female officers are involved in use of excessive force at rates substantially below those of male officers. Those statistics, as confirmed by both academic studies and anecdotal evidence, also indicate that women officers perform at least as well as their male counterparts when measured by traditional standards.

The Commission believes that the Chief of Police must seek tangible ways, for example, through the use of the discipline system, to establish the principle that racism and bias based on ethnicity, gender, or sexual orientation will not be tolerated within the Department. Racism and bias cannot be eliminated without active leadership from the top. Minority and female officers must be given full and equal opportunity to assume leadership positions in the LAPD. They must be assigned on a fully nondiscriminatory basis to the more desirable, "coveted" positions and promoted on the same nondiscriminatory basis to supervisory and managerial positions.

Community policing

The LAPD has an organizational culture that emphasizes crime control over crime prevention and that isolates the police from the communities and the people they serve. With the full support of many, the LAPD insists on aggressive detection of major crimes and a rapid, seven-minute response time to calls for service. Patrol officers are evaluated by statistical measures (for example, the number of calls handled and arrests made) and are rewarded for being "hardnosed." This style of policing produces results, but it does so at the risk of creating a siege mentality that alienates the officer from the community.

Witness after witness testified to unnecessarily aggressive confrontations between LAPD officers and citizens, particularly members of minority communities. From the statements of these citizens, as well as many present and former senior LAPD officers, it is apparent that too many LAPD patrol officers view citizens with resentment and hostility; too many treat the public with rudeness and disrespect. LAPD officers themselves seem to recognize the extent of the problem: nearly two-thirds (62.9%) of the 650 officers who responded to the recent LAPD survey expressed the opinion that "increased interaction with the community would improve the Department's relations with citizens."

Many FTOs [field training officers] openly perpetuate the siege mentality that alienates patrol officers from the community.

A model of community policing has gained increased acceptance in other parts of the country during the past ten years. The community policing model places service to the public and prevention of crime as the primary role of police in society and emphasizes problem solving, with active citizen involvement in defining those matters that are important to the community, rather than arrest statistics. Officers at the patrol level are required to spend less time in their cars communicating with other officers and more time on the street communicating with citizens. Proponents of this style of policing insist that addressing the causes of crime makes police officers more effective crimefighters and at the same time enhances the quality of life in the neighborhood.

The LAPD made early efforts to incorporate community policing principles and has continued to experiment with those concepts. For example, the LAPD's nationally recognized DARE [Drug Abuse Resistance Education] program has been viewed by officers and the public alike as a major achievement. The LAPD remains committed, however, to its traditional style of law enforcement with an emphasis on crime control and arrests. LAPD officers are encouraged to command and to confront, not to communicate. Community policing concepts, if successfully implemented, offer the prospect of effective crime prevention and substantially improved community relations. Although community-based policing is not a panacea for the problem of crime in society, the LAPD should carefully implement this model on a citywide basis. This will require a fundamental change in values. The Department must recognize the merits of community involvement in matters that affect local neighborhoods, develop programs to gain an adequate understanding of what is important to particular communities, and learn to manage departmental affairs in ways that are consistent with the community views expressed. Above all, the Department must understand that it is accountable to all segments of the community.

Recruitment

Although 40% of the candidates for admission to the Police Academy are disqualified as a result of psychological testing and background investigation, the Commission's review indicated that the initial psychological evaluation is an ineffective predictor of an applicant's tendencies toward violent behavior and that the background investigation pays too little attention to a candidate's history of violence. Experts agree that the best predictor of future behavior is previous behavior. Thus, the background investigation offers the best hope of screening out violence-prone applicants. Unfortunately, the background investigators are overworked and inadequately trained.

Improved screening of applicants is not enough. Police work modifies behavior. Many emotional and psychological problems may develop during an officer's tenure on the force. Officers may enter the force well suited psychologically for the job, but may suffer from burnout, alcohol-related problems, cynicism, or disenchantment, all of which can result in poor control over their behavior. A person's susceptibility to the behavior-modifying experiences of police work may not be revealed during even the most skilled and sophisticated psychological evaluation process. Accordingly, officers should be retested periodically to determine both psychological and physical problems. In addition, supervisors must understand their role to include training and counseling officers to cope with the problems policing can often entail, so that they may be dealt with before an officer loses control or requires disciplinary action.

Training

LAPD officer training has three phases. Each recruit spends approximately six months at the Police Academy. The new officer then spends one year on probation working with more experienced patrol officers who serve as field training officers (FTOs). Thereafter, all officers receive continuing training, which includes mandatory field training and daily training at roll call. The Commission believes that in each phase of the training additional emphasis is needed on the use of verbal skills rather than physical force to control potentially volatile situations and on the development of human relationship skills.

The quality of instruction at the Police Academy is generally impressive. However, at present the curriculum provides only eight hours in cultural awareness training. No more than one and one-half hours is devoted to any ethnic group. Substantially more training on this important topic is essential. In addition, the Academy's current Spanish language program needs to be reviewed and current deficiencies corrected. Officers with an interest in developing broader language skills should be encouraged to do so.

Upon graduation the new officer works as a "probationary officer" assigned to various field training officers. The FTOs guide new officers' first contacts with citizens and have primary responsibility for introducing the probationers to the culture and traditions of the Department. The Commission's interviews of FTOs in four representative divisions revealed that many FTOs openly perpetuate the siege mentality that alienates patrol officers from the community and pass on to their trainees confrontational attitudes of hostility and disrespect for the public. This problem is in part the result of flaws in the way FTOs are selected and trained. The hiring of a very large number of new officers in 1989, which required the use of less experienced FTOs, greatly exacerbated the problem.

Any officer promoted to Police Officer III by passing a written examination covering Department policies and procedures is eligible to serve as an FTO. At present there are no formal eligibility or disqualification criteria for the FTO position based on an applicant's disciplinary records.

Fourteen of the FTOs in the four divisions the Commission studied had been promoted to FTO despite having been disciplined for use of excessive force or use of improper tactics. There also appears to be little emphasis on selecting FTOs who have an interest in training junior officers, and an FTO's training ability is given little weight in his or her evaluation.

The most influential training received by a probationer comes from the example set by his or her FTO. Virtually all of the FTOs interviewed stated that their primary objective in training probationers is to instill good "officer safety skills." While the Commission recognizes the importance of such skills in police work, the probationers' world is quickly divided into "we/they" categories, [a situation that] is exacerbated by the failure to integrate any cultural awareness or sensitivity training into field training.

The Commission believes that, to become FTOs, officers should be required to pass written and oral tests designed to measure communications skills, teaching aptitude, and knowledge of Departmental policies regarding appropriate use of force, cultural sensitivity, community relations, and nondiscrimination. Officers with an aptitude for and interest in training junior officers should be encouraged by effective incentives to apply for FTO positions. In addition, the training program for FTOs should be modified to place greater emphasis on communication skills and the appropriate use of force. Successful completion of FTO School should be required before an FTO begins teaching probationers.

Promotion, assignment, and other personnel issues

In the civil service process for promotion of officers in the LAPD, the information considered includes performance evaluations, educational and training background, and all sustained complaints. The number and nature of any not sustained complaints, however, are not considered. The Commission recommends that a summary of not sustained complaints be considered in promotion decisions, as well as in paygrade advancements and assignments to desirable positions that are discretionary within the LAPD and outside the civil service system.

This is not to say that a past complaint history, even including a sustained complaint for excessive force, should automatically bar an officer from promotion. But there should be a careful consideration of the officer's complaint history including a summary of not sustained complaints, and particularly multiple complaints with similar fact patterns.

Complaint histories should also be considered in assignment of problem officers who may be using force improperly. For example, a problem officer can be paired with an officer with excellent communication skills that may lessen the need for use of force, as opposed to a partner involved in prior incidents of force with that problem officer. Another example is assignments to the jail facilities where potential for abuse by officers with a propensity to use excessive force is high. As several incidents examined by the Commission made clear, transfer of an officer to another geographical area is not likely to address a problem of excessive force without other remedial measures such as increased supervising, training and counseling.

Since 1980 the Department has permitted police officers working in patrol to select the geographic area or division for their patrol assignment subsequent to their initial assignment after completion of probation. As a result, sergeants and patrol officers tend to remain in one division for extended periods. The Commission believes that assignment procedures should be modified to require rotation through various divisions to ensure that officers work in a wide range of police functions and varied patrol locations during their careers. Such a rotation program will increase officers' experience and also will enable the Department to deploy police patrols with greater diversity throughout the City.

Under the current promotion system officers generally must leave patrol to advance within the Department. Notwithstanding the importance of the patrol function, therefore, the better officers are encouraged to abandon patrol. To give patrol increased emphasis and to retain good, experienced officers, the LAPD should increase rewards and incentives for patrol officers.

Personnel complaints and officer discipline

No area of police operations received more adverse comment during the Commission's public hearings than the Department's handling of complaints against LAPD officers, particularly allegations involving the use of excessive force. Statistics make the public's frustration understandable. Of the 2,152 citizen allegations of excessive force from 1986 through 1990, only 42 were sustained.

All personnel complaints are reviewed by a captain in the LAPD's Internal Affairs Division (IAD) to determine whether the complaint will be investigated by IAD or the charged officer's division. Generally IAD investigates only a few cases because of limited resources. Wherever investigated, the matter is initially adjudicated by the charged officer's division commanding officer, with a review by the area and bureau commanders.

The Commission has found that the complaint system is skewed against complainants. People who wish to file complaints face significant hurdles. Some intake officers actively discourage filing by being uncooperative or requiring long waits before completing a complaint form. In many heavily Latino divisions, there is often no Spanish speaking officer available to take complaints.

People who wish to file complaints face significant hurdles.

Division investigations are frequently inadequate. Based on a review of more than 700 complaint investigation files, the Commission found many deficiencies. For example, in a number of complaint files the Commission reviewed, there was no indication that the investigators had attempted to identify or locate independent witnesses or, if identified, to interview them. IAD investigations, on the whole, were of a higher quality than the division investigations. Although the LAPD has a special "officer involved shooting team," the Commission also found serious flaws in the investigation of shooting cases. Officers are frequently interviewed as a group, and statements are often not recorded until the completion of a "pre-interview."

The process of complaint adjudication is also flawed. First, there is no uniform basis for categorizing witnesses as "independent" or "non-involved" as opposed to "involved," although that distinction can determine whether a complaint is "not sustained" or "sustained." Some commanding officers also evaluate witnesses' credibility in inconsistent and biased ways that improperly favor the officer. Moreover, even when excessive force complaints are sustained, the punishment is more lenient than it should be. As explained by one deputy chief, there is greater punishment for conduct that embarrasses the Department (such as theft or drug use) than for conduct that reflects improper treatment of citizens. Statistical data also support the inference that the Department treats excessive force violations more leniently than it treats other types of officer misconduct.

Perhaps the greatest single barrier to the effective investigation and adjudication of complaints is the officers' unwritten code of silence: an officer does not provide adverse information against a fellow officer. While loyalty and support are necessary qualities, they cannot justify the violation of an officer's public responsibilities to ensure compliance with the law, including LAPD regulations.

A major overhaul of the disciplinary system is necessary to correct these problems. The Commission recommends creation of the Office of the Inspector General within the Police Commission with responsibility to oversee the disciplinary process and to participate in the adjudication and punishment of the most serious cases. The Police Commission should be responsible for overseeing the complaint intake process. Citizens must believe they can lodge complaints that will be investigated and determined fairly. All complaints relating to excessive force (including improper tactics) should be investigated by IAD, rather than at the involved officer's division, and should be subject to periodic audits by the Inspector General. While the Chief of Police should remain the one primarily responsible for imposing discipline in individual cases, the Police Commission should set guidelines as a matter of policy and hold the Chief accountable for following them.

3

Corruption in the New York City Police Department

Commission to Investigate Allegations of Police Corruption and the Anti-Corruption Procedures of the New York City Police Department

The Commission to Investigate Allegations of Police Corruption and the Anti-Corruption Procedures of the New York City Police Department, chaired by Milton Mollen, was formed in July 1992 by then-Mayor of New York City David N. Dinkins following the arrest of six New York City police officers for dealing narcotics.

The Commission (popularly known as the Mollen Commission) found that the nature of corruption in the New York City Police Department (NYPD) has changed in the last twenty years. As a result of the explosive growth of the crack cocaine trade, police officers are no longer merely taking bribes to look the other way but often are themselves committing major drug-related crimes. Police corruption is most prevalent in minority communities, where it exacerbates the existing problem of distrust between police and the community and undermines the department's hopes for its community policing programs. Police brutality must also be addressed in connection with corruption, since a willingness to use or tolerate brutality may demonstrate a willingness to engage in or tolerate corruption. Within the top management of the NYPD, the Commission found a neglect of supervisory functions and a pervasive belief that tolerating corruption was preferable to the scandal that would have resulted from exposing it. The NYPD's anti-corruption controls, put in place twenty years ago, failed over time as a result of this attitude among police management. The Commission therefore recommends strengthening internal anti-corruption controls and establishing a permanent external monitor to assess the NYPD's anticorruption efforts.

For the past century, police corruption inquiries into the New York City Police Department have run in twenty-year cycles of scandal, reform, backslide, and fresh scandal. The creation of this Commission followed the same historical pattern.

Commission to Investigate Allegations of Police Corruption and the Anti-Corruption Procedures of the New York City Police Department, Milton Mollen, chairman, *Interim Report and Principal Recommendations*, December 27, 1993. Reprinted with permission.

In May 1992, six New York City police officers assigned to two different Brooklyn precincts were arrested not by the New York City Police Department's Internal Affairs Division (IAD), but by Suffolk County [New York] Police. The officers were charged with narcotics crimes that arose from their association with a drug ring in Suffolk County.

Shortly thereafter, the press disclosed that one of the arrested officers, Michael Dowd, had been the subject of fifteen corruption allegations received by the New York City Police Department over a period spanning six years—and that not a single allegation ever had been proven by the Department, despite substantial evidence that Dowd regularly and openly engaged in serious criminal conduct. Questions arose as to whether Dowd was an aberration or whether corruption had once again become a serious problem within the Department, and whether the Department was able and willing to police itself.

In July 1992, Mayor David N. Dinkins responded by establishing this Commission and assigning it three tasks of deep public concern: to investigate the nature and extent of corruption in the Department; to evaluate the Department's procedures for preventing and detecting corruption; and to recommend changes and improvements in those procedures.

In September 1992, with a twenty-person staff of attorneys and investigators, the Commission began its work. We embarked upon a wide-ranging investigation to determine whether the corruption of Michael Dowd and the Department's failure to apprehend him illustrated deeper problems about police corruption and culture, and about the Department's competence and commitment to control corruption.

Anti-corruption efforts were more committed to avoiding disclosure of corruption than to preventing, detecting and uprooting it.

To carry out our mandate, the Commission sought information from a wide variety of sources. We reviewed thousands of Department documents and case files; conducted hundreds of private hearings and interviews of former and current police officers of all ranks; audited, investigated, and conducted performance tests of the principal components of the Department's anti-corruption systems; analyzed hundreds of investigative and personnel files; interviewed private citizens, alleged victims of corruption, and criminal informants; conducted an extensive literature review on police corruption and prevention; and held a series of roundtable discussions and other meetings with a variety of police management and corruption experts including local, state and federal law-enforcement officials, prosecutors, former and current police chiefs and commissioners, inspectors general, academics, and police union officials.

The Commission also initiated a number of its own field investigations, sometimes in conjunction with local and federal prosecutors, targeting areas where our analysis suggested police corruption existed.

The Commission received invaluable assistance from numerous police officers and supervisors who agreed to act as confidential sources of information about the state of the Department's corruption controls and investigations, including IAD investigators and supervisors, and undercover and field associate officers. Nine corrupt officers, including Michael

Dowd, provided the Commission with detailed information about their own and other officers' corrupt activities. A number of honest officers also provided information about corruption in their commands.

Throughout our work, we benefited from the counsel of many people, including Mark H. Moore and David M. Kennedy of Harvard University's John F. Kennedy School of Government, and Special Counsel Jonny J. Frank.

During the course of its investigation, the Commission developed extensive evidence about the state of police corruption in our City, the state of the Department's corruption controls, and the Department's ability and willingness to control corruption. From September 27 through October 7, 1993, the Commission held two weeks of public hearings to present much of the information we had uncovered in the primary areas of our mandate.

From the beginning of our investigation, we were struck by the difference between what the Commission was uncovering about the state of corruption and corruption controls within the Department, and what the Department was publicly—and privately—stating about itself. The Department maintained that police corruption was not a serious problem, and consisted primarily of sporadic, isolated incidents. It also insisted that the shortcomings that had been disclosed about the Department's anti-corruption efforts reflected, at worst, insufficient resources and uncoordinated organization of internal investigations.

The Commission found that the corruption problems facing the Department are far more serious than top commanders in the Department would admit. We determined that police corruption and brutality are serious problems, and that narcotics-related corruption occurs, in varying degrees, in many high-crime, narcotics-ridden precincts in our City. We also found an anti-corruption apparatus that was totally ineffective and—worse—a Department that was unable and unwilling to acknowledge and uncover the scope of police corruption. As a result, the Department's anti-corruption efforts were more committed to avoiding disclosure of corruption than to preventing, detecting and uprooting it.

Twenty years ago police officers took bribes to accommodate criminals . . . today's corrupt cop often is the criminal.

This institutional reluctance to acknowledge and uncover corruption is not surprising. Few organizations act otherwise. Police organizations in particular find it difficult to maintain an effective fight against corruption. It is unrealistic to expect the Department to exert a serious, effective, and sustained anti-corruption effort without outside help and oversight.

The very history of the Department lends weight to this conclusion. Despite cycles of scandal and reform spanning over a century, none has led to effective long-term remedies. The Commission is neither so naive nor optimistic to suggest that any reforms could ever entirely eliminate police corruption—or corruption in any profession. But we are convinced that there are reforms that can permanently strengthen the Department's corruption controls, and that can help break the twenty-year cycles of scandal and reform to which the Department has been captive.

One such critical reform, which is the principal recommendation addressed in this report, is the creation of a permanent outside agency to monitor and improve the Department's capacity for preventing and pursuing corruption, and to ensure the Mayor, Police Commissioner, and the public that the Department's anti-corruption efforts do not again erode with time. Enhancing the Department's internal efforts to prevent and uncover corruption, of course, is also critical, and we will make recommendations as to how this can be done in our final report.

What follows is an interim report summarizing the Commission's findings and recommendations for external oversight. The Commission's basic findings have become sufficiently clear, its principal recommendations sufficiently well developed, and the situation in the Department and the City sufficiently serious that the Commission feels called upon to issue an interim report at this time. Detailed findings and recommendations, including evidence generated by the Commission's pending investigations, will be presented in our final report, which will be released in June 1994.

The nature and extent of police corruption

The corruption of Michael Dowd was not isolated or aberrational, but represents a new and serious form of corruption that exists in a number of precincts throughout our City. While the systemic and institutionalized bribery schemes that plagued the Department a generation ago no longer exist, the prevalent forms of police corruption today exhibit an even more invidious and violent character: police officers assisting and profiting from drug traffickers, committing larceny, burglary, and robbery, conducting warrantless searches and seizures, committing perjury and falsifying statements, and brutally assaulting citizens.[1] This corruption is characterized by abuse and extortion, rather than by accommodation—principally through bribery—typical of traditional police corruption.

Simply put, twenty years ago police officers took bribes to accommodate criminals—primarily bookmakers; today's corrupt cop often is the criminal. Because of its aggressive and extortionate character, this form of corruption is particularly destructive to relations between the police and the public—which is especially troubling as the Department expands the practice of community policing.

The vast majority of police officers throughout our City do not engage in corruption. They are honest, hard-working men and women who perform difficult and dangerous duties each day with efficiency and integrity, doing their best to protect the people of our City. The horror many officers expressed at the revelations of the Commission's hearings was heartfelt and sincere.

Nonetheless, the Commission determined that corruption, particularly narcotics-related corruption, exists in varying degrees in many high-crime, drug-infested precincts in the City. This is based on the consistent and repeated results of the Commission's investigations; on information from sources within and without the Department; and on our analysis of patterns of corruption complaints. This corruption is not limited to the isolated acts of a few rogue cops, as some have maintained. It is typically committed by groups of police officers assigned to the same command who commit crimes under color of law; through the abuse, and with the protection of their police powers; and often in the shelter of their fellow officers' silence.

Nor is corruption limited to spontaneous crimes of opportunity, as many believe. Corrupt officers create their own opportunities for corruption. They aggressively seek out sources of money, drugs and guns, and often employ sophisticated and organized methods to carry out their criminal activities.

The Commission also found that the most serious and abusive corruption is endemic to crime-ridden, narcotics-infested precincts with predominantly minority populations. These communities are thus doubly victimized: by active trafficking in drugs and guns by the police themselves, and by being denied the police protection and service they so badly need.

Victims of police corruption are often reluctant to complain to the Department, which makes it difficult to uncover, investigate and determine the extent of corruption. This difficulty is augmented by other factors which make police corruption particularly difficult to uncover and investigate, including corruption's often covert and sophisticated nature, and the close ties of loyalty among the officers who perpetrate or witness it.

The Commission found no evidence that this corruption reached high into the Department, or that supervisors were actively and directly involved. Some supervisors do, however, appear to condone perjury, falsification of police records, and acts of brutality. They also facilitate corruption by often closing their eyes to corruption in their commands. Some supervisors knew or should have known about corruption and failed to take the actions necessary to stop it. But even supervisors committed to fighting corruption could not always do so. The Department failed to give supervisors the tools or incentives required to fight corruption effectively, and supervision was notably sparse and ineffective in most precincts where corruption flourished.

Finally, the traditional idea that police corruption is primarily about illicit profit no longer fully reflects what the Commission found on the streets of New York. While greed is still the primary cause of corruption, a complex array of other motivations also spurs corrupt officers: to exercise power; to experience thrills; to vent frustration and hostility; to administer street justice; and to win acceptance from fellow officers. Officers stole guns and drugs not only for profit, but in some instances to show their power, express their frustrations and impose their brand of justice. Officers sometimes used force for legitimate self-defense reasons, but also to steal money or drugs, to teach a lesson that officers believed the courts would not provide, or simply for power and thrills.

Police culture

What follows is a summary of police attitudes that foster and conceal corruption, and some of the most salient forms of corruption observed by the Commission.

The values and attitudes of police officers enormously influence the presence or absence of corruption and the ability to combat it. Certain tendencies promote corruption, or a tolerance for it. An intense group loyalty, fostered by pride, shared experiences, and a pervasive belief that police can rely only on other police in times of emergency, binds officers together. While loyalty and mutual trust are necessary and honorable aspects of police work, they can generate what is perhaps the greatest barrier to effective corruption control: the code of silence, the unwritten rule that an officer never gives incriminating information against a fellow officer.

The code of silence influences a vast number of police officers, even those who are otherwise honest. Officers who violate the code of silence often face severe consequences. They are ostracized and harassed; become targets of complaints and even physical threats; and fear that they will be left on their own when they most need help on the street. Consequently, many honest officers take no action to stop the wrongdoing they know or suspect is taking place around them. The code of silence also often extends to supervisors, who seek to protect their subordinates from charges of misconduct and their own careers from the taint of scandal.

Another aspect of police culture is the "us versus them" mentality that many police display and which is at its worst in high-crime, predominantly minority precincts. This divisiveness makes many police officers feel isolated from, and often hostile toward, the community they are meant to serve. The Commission's inquiries show that this attitude starts as early as the police academy, where impressionable recruits learn from veteran police officers that the ordinary citizen fails to appreciate the police, and that their safety depends solely on fellow officers. This attitude is powerfully reinforced on the job. It creates strong pressures on police officers to ally themselves with fellow officers, even corrupt ones, and to disregard the interest they have in supportive, productive relationships with the communities and residents they serve.

Corrupt officers create their own opportunities for corruption.

Police unions and fraternal organizations can do much to change the attitudes of their members. Because of this, we were particularly disappointed when the Patrolmen's Benevolent Association (PBA) declined our invitation to discuss this matter. Moreover, a variety of sources, including police officers and prosecutors, have reported that police unions help perpetuate the characteristics of police culture that foster corruption. In particular, the Commission learned that delegates of the PBA have attempted to thwart law-enforcement efforts into police corruption. Rather than acting to protect the legitimate interests of the vast majority of its honest members, the PBA often acts as a shelter for officers who commit acts of misconduct.

The code of silence and the "us versus them" mentality were present wherever we found corruption. These characteristics of police culture largely explain how groups of corrupt officers, sometimes comprising almost an entire squad, can openly engage in corruption for long periods of time with impunity. Any successful system for corruption control must redirect police culture against protecting and perpetuating police corruption. It must create a culture that demands integrity and works to ensure it. The Commission believes such change is possible.

History proves that our optimism is warranted. In response to the Knapp Commission's revelations [in 1972] of systemic corruption and corruption tolerance, then-Commissioner Patrick V. Murphy made significant strides in transforming a culture that committed and tolerated corruption into one that largely discouraged it. Then, as now, the Department could be divided into three camps: a few determined offenders, a few determined incorruptibles, and a large group in the middle who could be tilted either way, and who are, at the moment, tilted toward corruption tolerance. As it did twenty years ago, the Department must take a variety of steps to reverse this inclination by: emphasizing and spreading the system of "command accountability" and incentives for preventing corruption; strengthening the corruption prevention and investigations apparatus; and inculcating an ideology of pride and integrity throughout the Department.

Any successful plan for reform has to rely heavily on steps to create a culture that discourages corruption. If the culture of the Department tolerates corruption, or conceals it, no systems of prevention and investigation are likely fully to succeed. But if the culture demands integrity and works to ensure it, those systems will be more productive.

Narcotics-related corruption

The most serious corruption problems within the Department arise from the narcotics trade. The traditional unwritten rule of twenty years ago that narcotics graft is "dirty money" has disappeared. The explosion of the cocaine and crack trade that began in the 1980s provides police officers with plentiful opportunities to steal money, drugs, and other property from drug dealers who are unlikely to complain, and to associate with drug dealers who will pay handsomely for police protection.

Unlike a generation ago, when narcotics corruption was confined to units of plainclothes narcotics officers, today's narcotics corruption primarily involves the uniformed patrol force. Nonetheless, even the most elite units of the Department are not immune to narcotics corruption. For example, two detectives assigned to the New York Drug Enforcement Task Force recently pleaded guilty and were convicted of drug trafficking charges in connection with their attempt to sell narcotics lawfully seized in a large-scale narcotics investigation.

Police officers profit from the narcotics trade in a variety of ways, from petty thefts and shakedowns of street dealers to using their police powers to protect and assist large-scale drug organizations in return for sizeable payoffs. The primary forms of narcotics-related corruption we discovered—which officers often carried out while on duty and in uniform—include the following:

- Providing assistance and protection to narcotics organizations for payoffs, including selling confidential information, providing protection for transportation of drugs and drug money, harassing competitive dealers, and becoming active entrepreneurs in drug rackets;
- Thefts, sometimes violent, of drugs, money, and firearms from drug dealers;
- Thefts of drugs, money and property seized as evidence;
- Robberies of drug dealers;
- Burglaries of drug locations;
- Selling narcotics, which officers often obtained through theft or as payment from dealers, including sales to other officers, or dealers from whom the drugs were stolen; and
- Selling illegally seized weapons—including sales of guns to drug dealers.

Narcotics corruption rarely involves a single police officer taking advantage of an isolated opportunity to "score" money, drugs, or both. Rather, it usually involves groups of police officers, acting with various degrees of organization, actively seeking opportunities to score from drug dealers through protection rackets, larceny, extortion, burglary, or robbery.

The explosion of the cocaine and crack trade . . . provides police officers with plentiful opportunities to steal money, drugs, and other property.

One Commission investigation, for example, revealed a group of ten to twelve patrol officers assigned to a Brooklyn precinct who, for at least two years, regularly broke into drug locations to steal money, drugs, and firearms. They communicated with each other by using code names over Department radios to arrange clandestine meetings and to plan their illegal raids. Once they had selected a location, they assigned each other roles to perform in the raid and later split stolen cash either in or around the stationhouse or at secret off-duty locations. Similar patterns exist in other precincts as well.

Narcotics corruption among police officers does not end with efforts to score from the drug trade. Personal drug use, especially the use of cocaine and steroids, has also become a significant problem among police officers, even those who may not otherwise engage in other kinds of wrongdoing. While the Commission continues to inquire into the extent of this problem, information from corrupt officers, honest officers, and Department health services officials indicates that the problem has grown over recent years, spurring the Department to significantly increase the frequency of random drug tests in 1993.

Police violence

Police corruption investigations typically ignore police violence. This Commission rejected that traditional course because we found that police violence is a serious problem confronting the Department, and may indicate an officer's willingness to engage in corruption. The traditional distinction between corruption and brutality, therefore, no longer applies. Thus any investigation of corruption would be remiss in overlooking brutality.

A number of officers have told us that they were "broken in" to the world of corruption by committing acts of brutality; it was their first step toward other kinds of corruption. A willingness to abuse people in custody or others who challenge police authority can be a way to prove that an officer is a tough cop who can be trusted and accepted by fellow officers. Brutality, like other kinds of misconduct, thus sometimes serves as a rite of initiation into aspects of police culture that foster corruption.

No one would deny that the use of force is often a necessity—and indeed often crucial to protect an officer's life in the line of duty. We found, however, that the use of force sometimes exceeds the bounds of necessity. Some police officers use violence gratuitously: to demonstrate their preeminence on the streets; to administer on-the-spot retribution for crimes they believe will go unpunished by the courts; and for power and thrills. We also found that such behavior is widely tolerated in the Department.

The Civilian Complaint Review Board is responsible for investigating excessive force allegations. However, the Department has failed to carry out its duty to aggressively prevent and uncover acts of brutality, to hold supervisors accountable for failing to pursue signs of unnecessary violence on their watch, and to solicit information about brutality from other officers or the public.

Perjury, false statements and records

Falsifying Department records and making false statements is not uncommon among certain police officers, even among those who do not engage in other kinds of misconduct. Most often, police falsifications are made to justify an unlawful arrest or search that would otherwise not survive in court, especially in cases of drug or firearms possession; to conceal other corrupt activities; or to excuse the use of excessive force.

Police officers also falsify records to inflate arrest numbers, to enhance arrest charges, to allow seizure of otherwise unseizable evidence, to increase overtime, and to defend their own conduct and the conduct of fellow officers in corruption and excessive force investigations. Superior officers often do little to deter these practices. Indeed, in at least one case, a superior officer went so far as to direct subordinates to falsify official reports for self-serving or, for what were believed to be, legitimate law-enforcement purposes.

The consequences of perjury and falsification can be devastating. It can mean that defendants are unlawfully arrested and convicted, that inadmissible evidence is admitted at trial, and ultimately the public trust in even the most honest officer is eroded. This erosion of trust causes the public to disbelieve police testimony resulting in the guilty being set free after trial.

The failures of the Department's corruption controls

The Commission found a deep-rooted institutional reluctance to uncover corruption in the Department. This was not surprising. Powerful forces discourage the Department from sustaining efforts to uncover corruption—which is why an external force is needed to maintain a sense of commitment and accountability.

Police managers ask a great deal of their officers. They ask them to be alert, ready, and available to respond to whatever citizens demand from them; to be courteous and fair no matter how offensive or provocative the behavior of the citizens they encounter; and to be ever willing to face danger to protect the people of our City. Because they must ask for so much from their officers, they rightly judge that they should offer trust, support and loyalty in exchange.

Unfortunately, one of the easiest ways that the Department can show trust and support for its officers is to be less than zealous in efforts to control and uncover corruption. Pursuing corruption—taking the complaints of citizens (even drug dealers) seriously, using tough investigative methods to determine the truth of allegations, and using pro-active measures to search out corruption—will be perceived by some as a lack of trust and thus lower morale.

The top management of the Department also understands that revelations of corruption will be dealt with harshly in the court of public opinion. When corruption is uncovered, the press and the public invariably take it as a symptom of a larger problem and a failure of management. Thus, police commanders perceive that their careers may be harmed and that public confidence will erode, thus jeopardizing the Department's effectiveness in fighting crime.

As a result, top management believed that it would get no reward, and pay a heavy price, for vigilance against corruption. It is no wonder that over time the Department tends to relax its vigilance, and may even throw up roadblocks to uncovering corruption.

Without constant management attention to preventing corruption, however, corrupt officers feel they can act with impunity, honest officers are more vulnerable to the code of silence, and leadership is more easily drawn to other priorities.

This appears to have happened in the Department. From the top brass down to local precinct commanders and supervisors, there was a pervasive belief that uncovering serious corruption would harm careers and the reputation of the Department. There was a debilitating fear of the embarrassment and loss of public confidence that corruption headlines would bring.

As a result, avoiding scandal became more important than fighting corruption. Daniel Sullivan, the six-year chief of the Department's anti-corruption division, testified at the Commission's public hearings that:

> . . . the Department [was] paranoid over bad press. Everything that IAD did reflected poorly on the rest of the Department and generated bad press. So when I went up with the bad news that two cops were going to be arrested . . . I felt like they wanted to shoot me because I was always the bearer of the bad news. They were interested primarily in getting good press . . . there was a message that went out to the field that maybe we shouldn't be so aggressive in fighting corruption because the Department just does not want bad press.

Numerous officers expressed similar fears of exposing serious corruption.

The reluctance to uncover and effectively investigate corruption infected the entire anti-corruption apparatus, from training, supervision and command accountability to investigations and intelligence gathering. Our investigation revealed an anti-corruption system that was more likely to conceal corruption than uncover it, and a Department often more interested in the appearance of integrity than its reality. Oversight of anti-corruption efforts was virtually nonexistent; intelligence gathering efforts were negligible; corruption investigations were often deliberately limited and prematurely closed; and Integrity Control Officers and supervisors were denied the tools needed to uncover corruption and, in practice, played virtually no role in corruption control efforts.

And perhaps most alarming, in a Department known for its high levels of performance, investigative ingenuity, and managerial expertise, no one seemed to care. Despite the importance of its corruption-fighting mandate, the Department allocated little of its billion-dollar-plus budget to anti-corruption efforts. Moreover, although performance in most divisions in the Department is carefully scrutinized at several levels, neither IAD nor other units or supervisors responsible for fighting corruption were held accountable for their performance.

Nor did anyone in the Department know how the Department's anti-corruption efforts had been functioning until this Commission commenced its audit and investigation of the principal components of those anti-corruption efforts. What was known was that the Department's anti-corruption systems were not working well. But that was acceptable, if not preferable: ineffectiveness minimized the likelihood of embarrassment, scandal and a perceived loss of public confidence. Totally overlooked was the public's loss of confidence in the integrity of the Department and the debilitating impact upon the Department's moral fiber.

This is precisely why the past failures of the Department's anti-corruption efforts are so important—and illuminating. They show the inevitable consequence of leaving anti-corruption efforts and oversight solely within the control of the very Department that believes it will be embarrassed and harmed by the success of those efforts.

A brief summary of our preliminary findings on these failures follows.

The Department Abandoned Its Responsibility to Ensure Integrity: The Department failed to impress upon its members that fighting corruption must be one of the Department's highest priorities. The Department devoted insufficient resources, personnel, effort, and planning to preventing and uncovering corruption. Officers of all ranks told us that the general feeling in the Department was that it was better not to know about, much less report, corruption. A "see no evil, hear no evil" mentality often governed supervisors, patrol officers, and even corruption investigators.

The Department Failed to Address Aspects of Police Culture That Foster Corruption: Despite overwhelming evidence of a widespread tolerance of corruption and violence, the Department failed to address police attitudes and practices that foster corruption, and to inculcate attitudes that discourage it. Officers and supervisors were neither encouraged nor rewarded for taking stands against corruption; nor were penalties imposed for being silent or willfully blind to corruption; and officers and supervisors were rarely held accountable for corruption about which they were, or should have been, aware.

The Department Had a Fragmented Approach to Corruption Control: Combating police corruption requires a coherent, integrated strategy, and coordinated effort and attention on several fronts. These would include, at a minimum, intelligent recruitment; thorough training; effective supervision; strong accountability; thorough investigations; effective intelligence gathering and analysis; meaningful discipline; and vigilant oversight. The Department had no such integrated strategy, and the various parts of what should have been a coordinated system were either nonexistent or unproductive.

The System of "Command Accountability" Collapsed: A prime component of the Department's capacity to prevent and uncover corruption is the principle of command accountability: that all commanders are responsible for pursuing corruption in their commands; that they will be evaluated firmly but fairly on their anti-corruption performance; and will be furnished with the tools and resources necessary to do so. In the past, field commanders had Field Internal Affairs Units (FIAUs) to investigate corruption in their commands. The FIAUs were accountable both to the field commander and to IAD.

Only the skeleton of this system now remains. Its animating principle—that all commanders must act, and will be held accountable for acting, against corruption—has disappeared. There is a widespread perception among commanders and supervisors that uncovering corruption on their watch leads to punishment rather than reward.

We found a total lack of commitment to the principle of command accountability. This was allowed to happen because no formal institutional mechanisms were ever adopted to ensure its perpetuation and enforcement. Its success depended on the commitment of the Department's top commanders. When that commitment eroded, so too did the centerpiece of the Department's anti-corruption systems.

The Department Allowed the FIAUs to Collapse: Although the FIAUs were purportedly the backbone of the Department's investigative efforts, they were denied the resources and personnel required to do their job. Moreover, although the FIAUs depended largely on IAD's assistance and oversight, IAD rarely assisted or even cooperated with the FIAUs. In fact, IAD often thwarted FIAU investigations by withholding critical information and resources.

Even worse, the Department permitted IAD to use the FIAUs as a dumping ground for corruption allegations. IAD assigned the poorly resourced FIAUs a caseload that FIAU officers of all ranks testified was so overwhelming it was impossible to handle. As a result, a large number of corruption cases filed with the Department each year—including over a dozen investigations involving Michael Dowd—were closed as unsubstantiated without appropriate investigative steps ever having been taken.

The Internal Affairs Division Abandoned Its Mission: IAD abandoned its primary responsibilities to investigate serious and complex corruption cases; to uncover patterns of corruption through trend analysis and self-initiated investigations; and to oversee and assist the FIAUs. For example, IAD assigned itself a caseload of largely easy cases, including cases like sleeping on the job; failed to solicit significant information through its undercover program; initiated no self-generated investigations during at least the past five years, despite an entire unit purportedly dedicated to that task; and relied on a large number of investigators with no prior investigative experience, many of whom never took the required investigations training course. Consequently, as the Commission uniformly heard from officers of a variety of ranks, IAD was viewed with contempt by members of the Department and failed to serve as a deterrent to corruption.

The Department Used a Badly Flawed Investigative Approach for Police Corruption: Investigations into police corruption purposefully minimized the likelihood of uncovering the full extent of corruption. Interestingly, the Department's investigations excelled in every area except police corruption. The Commission uncovered a pattern of cases that were prematurely closed and failed to employ basic investigative techniques (like the use of undercovers, sting operations, and turn-arounds) that are routinely relied on in other investigative divisions of the Department. Moreover, IAD operated as a solely reactive investigative division that responded only to isolated complaints rather than patterns of corruption. IAD also fragmented what should have been large-scale investigations by sending out related allegations as separate investigations. Thus, IAD knowingly ignored opportunities to develop investigations of large-scale corruption.

Corruption Cases Were Concealed: IAD and the Inspectional Services Bureau Chief had unbridled discretion to control police corruption investigations and decide what allegations should be officially recorded and sent to prosecutors. We found evidence of abuse of that power. For example, certain corruption cases were kept out of IAD's regular filing system and concealed from prosecutors through a file called the "Tickler File."

The Department's Intelligence Gathering Efforts Were Flawed: The Department made virtually no effort to solicit information from the public, police officers, or other sources of information—even though such efforts are crucial to uncovering information about police corruption. The Department made little effort to generate information about corruption in the absence of a complaint. It rarely used directed integrity tests and often failed to pursue information from its own field associates, one of the Department's best resources for reliable information about corruption. The Department's complaint intake efforts also minimized the likelihood of obtaining information on corruption: The Department's "Action Desk"— which receives and processes information on police corruption—routinely discouraged individuals from providing information. Department statistics, therefore, vastly underestimate the nature and extent of corruption, and investigations reach only small portions of a much wider problem.

Avoiding scandal became more important than fighting corruption.

Supervision Was Diluted and Ineffective: Although effective first-line supervision is critical in the fight against corruption, few first-line supervisors perceived corruption control as an important responsibility. The Department did little to suggest otherwise. Even supervisors bent on ensuring integrity often lacked the resources or time to do so. In many precincts, supervisors were responsible for so many officers or so large an area that effective supervision was impossible. Department commanders often assigned supervisors without regard to prior experience, training, or the needs of the command. Inexperienced, probationary sergeants were often assigned to busy, corruption-prone precincts where experienced, proven supervisors are most needed. Thus, in many busy, crime-ridden precincts corrupt officers felt they had free rein. While no amount of supervision will stop all determined offenders, a reasonable level of committed supervision is essential to deter corruption.

Recruit and In-Service Integrity Training Was Neglected: Integrity training has been long neglected by the Department. Insufficient attention was devoted to integrity training at the Police Academy, and "required" in-service integrity training for officers and supervisors was often not provided. When training was offered, it relied largely on obsolete materials and films that remained largely unchanged since the days of the Knapp Commission and rarely captured serious attention either from recruits or veteran officers.

Effective Deterrence Was Absent: Effective general and specific deterrence was lacking. The likelihood of detection and punishment was minimal, as was the severity of the sanction imposed. Indeed, one method of dealing with corruption was simply to transfer problem officers to unattractive assignments, including crime-ridden precincts. This "dumping ground" method of discipline punishes the community more than the problem officers by assigning them to the very precincts where the opportunities for corruption most abound, where the need for talented, committed officers is the greatest, and where minority populations often reside.

Drug and Alcohol Abuse Policies Were Ineffective: Despite evidence of a serious drug and alcohol problem confronting the Department, little was done to prevent, treat, or uncover the full extent of this problem. Abuse problems are often ignored or mishandled, certain drug tests are given too infrequently, many testing procedures are easy to circumvent, and effective drug treatment is nonexistent.

Principal recommendations

Most of the failures of the Department's corruption controls could have been prevented, identified, or remedied years ago if the Department had been accountable to regular independent review of its anti-corruption systems. History strongly suggests that the erosion of the Department's corruption control efforts is an inevitable consequence of its institutional reluctance to uncover corruption—unless some countervailing power forces the Department to do what it naturally strays from doing. This is true of many organizations. It is unrealistic to expect otherwise from the Department. The mere establishment of this independent Commission created such a countervailing pressure, as did the creation of the Knapp Commission twenty years ago. After the creation of this Commission, [then-] Police Commissioner Raymond W. Kelly made a number of laudable reforms in the Department's anti-corruption apparatus. It is no coincidence that it was only under the scrutiny of oversight Commissions that there was a heightened vigilance and commitment to anti-corruption efforts in the Department. Our challenge is to sustain that vigilance so that history does not again repeat itself.

The Commission believes that the Department must remain responsible for effectively policing itself and for keeping its own house in order. This requires that the Department have effective internal corruption controls to prevent and uncover corruption. The Commission also believes that it is impossible for the Department to bear that responsibility alone. The Department is subject to powerful internal pressures to avoid uncovering corruption, which are almost certain to prevail absent external scrutiny.

The Commission therefore urges a dual-track approach to improving police corruption controls. The first track focuses on the Department's entire internal apparatus for the control of corruption. Police Commissioner Kelly has made important inroads to strengthening this internal apparatus, and he should be commended for his efforts. His principal reforms, however, focus largely on strengthening and centralizing investigative efforts, rather than on prevention, root causes, and conditions. The Commission's final report will make detailed recommendations for internal reforms on a variety of fronts, including:

- improving screening and recruitment;
- improving recruit education and in-service integrity training;
- attacking corruption and brutality tolerance;
- challenging other aspects of police culture and conditions that breed corruption and brutality;
- revitalizing and enforcing command accountability;
- strengthening first-line supervision;
- enhancing sanctions and disincentives for corruption and brutality;
- strengthening intelligence-gathering efforts;
- preventing, detecting and treating drug and alcohol abuse;
- soliciting police union support for anti-corruption efforts;
- minimizing the corruption hazards of community policing; and
- legislative reforms, including the issue of residency requirements.

The second track focuses on the creation of an independent, external monitor to ensure that the Department's commitment to preventing corruption is sustained and that its internal systems for pursuing corruption operate effectively. It is this external monitor that will be the focus of this interim report.

The external monitor

The Commission urges the immediate establishment of a permanent external monitor, independent of the Department, to assess the effectiveness of the Department's systems for detecting, preventing, and investigating corruption; to evaluate Department conditions and values that affect the incidence of police corruption; to conduct continual audits of the state of corruption within the Department; and, when appropriate, to make recommendations for improvement. The monitor will issue periodic reports on its findings and recommendations to the Mayor and the Police Commissioner.

This monitor will also serve as a management tool for the Police Commissioner. It will ensure that the Department's anti-corruption systems work effectively—and that under his or her tenure, the Department will not fall victim to the institutional pressures that erode anti-corruption efforts. The monitor will:

- ensure that the Department has effective methods for receiving and recording corruption allegations and analyzing corruption trends;
- assess the sufficiency and quality of investigative resources and personnel;
- ensure that the Department employs effective methods and management in conducting corruption investigations, including that it no longer solely relies on a reactive investigative system that narrowly focuses on isolated complaints and that rarely employs proactive investigative techniques;
- ensure that the Department has successful intelligence-gathering efforts, including effective undercover, field associate, integrity testing, and community outreach programs;
- evaluate the Department's efforts to revitalize and enforce command accountability;
- ensure that the Department strengthens supervision, including levels and quality of first-line supervision, training of supervisors, and consideration of integrity history in determining assignments and promotions;
- require the Department to produce reports on police corruption and corruption trends, including analysis of the number of complaints investigated and the disposition of those complaints, the number of arrests and referrals for prosecution, and the number of Department disciplinary proceedings and the sanctions imposed; and
- conduct performance tests and inspections of the Department's anti-corruption units and programs to guarantee that the Department continually maximizes its capacity to police itself.

The monitor must also have its own investigative capacity to successfully carry out its audits of the Department's internal controls. It will conduct its own self-initiated corruption investigations, intelligence-gathering efforts, and integrity tests to the extent necessary to test the Department's performance. This capacity is not meant to replace the Department's or prosecutors' own investigations or to serve an enforcement purpose, but to ensure that the Department's intelligence-gathering and investigative efforts are focused on areas where corruption is likely to exist.

This investigative capacity is crucial to successfully carrying out the monitor's principal task of auditing and evaluating the Department's anti-corruption efforts. It was only by having such an investigative capacity that this Commission was able to uncover many of the deficiencies in the Department's intelligence-gathering, investigative and supervisory efforts, and to determine that the nature and extent of corruption was far more serious than suggested by the Department's official position on corruption.

Monitoring cultural conditions

The monitor must also:

- ensure that the Department makes effective efforts to reform the conditions and attitudes that nurture and perpetuate corruption and brutality;
- assess the effectiveness of recruit education, integrity training, field training operation, and the integrity standards set by supervisors;
- ensure that the Department works to eliminate corruption and brutality tolerance and the code of silence;
- evaluate Department efforts to pursue and uncover brutality and its connection to corruption;
- determine whether the Department routinely assigns officers with discipline problems only to certain commands within the Department, such as high-crime, minority precincts, and determine the impact of such practices;
- evaluate the effectiveness of the Department's drug and alcohol abuse policies, and prevention, treatment, and detection efforts;
- evaluate the Department's efforts to overcome police attitudes that isolate them from the public and often create the appearance of a hostile and corrupt police force; and
- enhance liaison efforts with community groups and precinct community councils to provide the Department with input from the public about their perception and information about police corruption and to obtain information for the monitor's recommendations for reform.

We recommend that the Mayor establish a permanent Police Commission headed by three to five highly reputable and knowledgeable citizens appointed by the Mayor who would be willing to serve pro bono. We further recommend that the Commissioners have a limited, staggered term to guarantee turnover, avoid staleness, and prevent the development of a long-term bureaucratic relationship with the Department that could compromise the Commission's independence.

To accomplish its tasks, the Commission's powers should include: the power to subpoena witnesses and documents, unrestricted access to Department records and personnel; the power to administer oaths and take testimony in private and public hearings; and the power to grant use immunity. We do not recommend the creation of a large and costly bureaucracy. With the aforementioned powers, the Commission could perform its work with a small staff of people with varied expertise, including attorneys, investigators, police management experts, and organizational and statistical analysts.

The Police Commission should cooperate with the Police Commissioner in establishing a total commitment to maintaining integrity and the corruption-fighting capacity of the Department. It should monitor the implementation of a system of accountability throughout the Department enforced by a program of incentives and disincentives. The Police Commission should cooperate with the Police Commissioner in redefining police culture to reflect the identity of interest between the members of the public and the Department with emphasis on the infusion of mutual respect.

It is the Commission's hope that this interim report will assist the Mayor, the Police Commissioner, and the people of New York City in addressing the problems of police corruption, and the reforms necessary to combat it effectively today and in the future.

Notes

1. Corruption today is not limited to these types of crimes, as our final report will make clear. Some officers continue to accept and solicit gratuities from business owners, tow-truck operators and the like. These corrupt practices should not be ignored. As officers repeatedly told us, serious corruption often begins with more minor misconduct and corruption. This interim report, however, focuses only on the more serious forms of corruption we uncovered.

4

Community-Oriented Policing Would Prevent Police Brutality

Jerome H. Skolnick and James J. Fyfe

Jerome H. Skolnick is a law professor at the University of California, Berkeley, and has authored or collaborated on many works on law enforcement and juvenile delinquency. James J. Fyfe, a former New York City police officer, is now a professor of criminal justice at Temple University and is the author of several books on policing.

Community-oriented policing and problem-oriented policing are new remedies for excessive use of force by police. Traditional, professional policing strategy, with police in radio cars responding to 911 calls, has failed to reduce crime and has promoted a culture of brutality, undermining relations between police and citizens. Implementing community-oriented policing—with a decentralized command structure to allow greater community involvement and interaction with police—requires not only a commitment by police chiefs, but a reform of the attitudes of patrol officers. Problem-oriented policing is designed to make police more flexible and to allow them to respond to underlying problems in high-crime areas, reducing recurrences of crime and making citizens feel safer.

Two emerging philosophies—*community-oriented policing* and *problem-oriented policing*—have recently attempted to systematize the concept of broadening input into police policy that was pioneered by [Hans] Toch and his colleagues. Under the label "community-oriented policing" such notions as police–community reciprocity, decentralization of command, reorientation of patrol, and generalized rather than specialized policing are commending themselves to police executives around the globe.[1] At first thought this is quite surprising. Why should police executives in places with such different cultures, different economies, and different traditions as Oslo [Norway], Tokyo, London, New York, and Santa Ana [California] be advocating similar reforms? After all, London is perhaps the world's most diverse and cosmopolitan metropolis, not unlike New York, while Santa Ana has a population about the size of a London borough, located 33 miles southeast of Los Angeles, and Oslo is the relatively small capital (750,000) of a homogeneously populated Scandinavian welfare state.

The answer seems to be that with respect to crime—and perhaps even more to fear of crime arising from public disorder (what sociologist Albert Reiss, Jr., has called "soft crime")[2]—there has developed an almost international language, a virtually reflexive set of public reactions. One part of the response is to impose heavier and mandated sentences on convicted criminals, to fill the jails and prisons to capacity and overcapacity. However mistrusted police might be, another part is to look to the police to prevent crime and public disorder.

The failure of traditional policing

Which leads to a larger question: Is it possible for police to prevent crime from occurring in the first place? There is some evidence that police can prevent specific offenses, but no one really knows how much police can contribute to crime prevention in the aggregate, especially since police researchers and managers have learned how unsuccessful traditional crime-fighting strategies by police were during the 1970s and 1980s. That is mainly why the new hope is in "community-oriented policing," a strategy that directs police resources away from traditional responses and attempts to foster a partnership between the "community" and the organization and direction of policing. Community-oriented policing has become widespread, prevalent, and fashionable not because it has been proved to work, but because the alternatives to it have been proved to fail. The most glaring recent failure has been the aggressive style of the Los Angeles Police Department (LAPD), of which the Rodney King beating is just one symptom.

Police executives have come to recognize other failures of strategy as well. One is to throw money and technology at the crime problem. But police managers, informed by criminal justice researchers, have learned that hiring more police does not necessarily result in less crime or increase the proportion of crimes solved. The same can be said for enlarging police budgets or licensing police to be *aggressive* in their prevention efforts. The most that can be warranted is that, if cops were to disappear entirely, there would be more crime. But once a certain threshold of police department size has been reached—long ago met in most major cities—neither more police nor more money helps much. Variations in crime, clearance rates [the rates at which crimes are "solved"], and public disorder are related to such stubbornly intractable factors as income, levels of employment, education, and population heterogeneity. Throwing money at law enforcement offers no solution to these larger persistent social factors that are so highly correlated with crime. Besides, in the declining budget climate of the 1990s, there isn't much money to throw at either police or social problems. Hence, the search for a new approach to policing.

Police managers also have learned that random motorized patrolling neither reduces crime nor improves the chances of catching suspects. It used to be thought that saturating an area with patrol cars would prevent crime. It does seem to—but only temporarily—largely by displacing crime to other areas. Yet even when police inundate an area, they rarely see a crime in progress. That happens sometimes, but mostly in the movies, as when Dirty Harry has his lunch disturbed by an armed robbery. Regular patrols by officers on foot have not been demonstrated to reduce crime either, but they do raise public confidence in the safety of the streets. The incident-driven patrol car, visible to citizens mainly when it is en route to calls for service, does not appear to offer similar reassurance.[3]

Nor does slicing response time to crime incidents—a hallmark of police management in the 1970s—raise the likelihood of arresting the criminal or satisfying the crime victim. One major study showed an initially surprising but commonsensical finding—the chances of making an arrest on the spot drops below ten percent if even one minute elapses from the time the crime is committed.[4] But even if cops could move with the speed of comic book heroes, in a flash, it would not matter. Crime victims delay an average of four to five and one-half minutes before picking up a telephone to report the crime. After such a delay, how fast the police respond is irrelevant. And there cannot even be a response time when a woman is too afraid or embarrassed to report a beating or a rape because of the treatment she expects from police.

Researchers have learned that police who ride in patrol cars, especially two-person cars, become rather self-contained and remote, neither reassuring citizens enough to reduce their fear of crime nor engendering trust. In fact, except perhaps in the most congested areas, where it is very difficult for solo patrol officers to drive and observe the sidewalks at the same time, there is really no objective need for the two-person car. Studies have shown that police are no more likely to be injured in one-person patrol cars. And two-person patrol cars are no more effective in catching criminals or reducing crime.[5] Oddly enough, this lesson has been learned in some American cities, even in places like Oakland, California, with its machine-gun-toting drug dealers and record homicide rates. But in Europe, even in peaceful Scandinavia, police regard the companionship of the two-person car as an indispensable component of the job. We suspect that it is for these same reasons of companionship—rather than for considerations of safety or effectiveness—that police officers in some American cities fight tooth-and-nail to retain two-person cars.

These research findings are nothing short of devastating to earlier assumptions of managerial professionalism and incident-driven (911-driven) policing, which—to the horror of specialists in time management rather than policing—puts the development of police in the hands of an amorphous and faceless public. To the thoughtful police administrator, the findings suggest that traditional patrol strategies are neither reducing crime nor reassuring potential crime victims, some of whom fear the police as much as they do the criminals. Thinking police professionals have had to develop some new ideas. Community-oriented policing is the leading one.

Community-oriented policing

Community-oriented policing is not a detailed, coherent program whose elements can be checked off by a novice chief assuming the job. Above all, it is a philosophy of policing, a new professionalism, which cannot succeed without a chief's energetic and abiding commitment to democratic, rather than technocratic, values. It is almost a new vision of the role of police in a democratic society. A Norwegian government report expresses the essence of this philosophy when it says that "the police are able to carry out their tasks satisfactorily only through constructive cooperation with the public."[6] Under this philosophy, the chief is responsible for generating a new normative climate—not easy to accomplish—which will assume that ordinary citizens have a contribution to make to the policing enterprise, that they are partners in the production of social order.

The distinction between traditional professionalism and democratic professionalism was made nicely by a Santa Ana, California, businessman who was asked about what had changed with the introduction of community-oriented policing to the Santa Ana Police Department (SAPD). The businessman said that when the city hired community-oriented administrator Raymond Davis to be Chief of Police, they were looking for a police executive who was "up to date," who combined management expertise and technological sophistication with an ability to relate to the broader community. The same businessman continued, "We wanted someone who was willing to work together with the residential and business communities. The old guard didn't want to hear from the community. They told us they were professionals and that they didn't want to have anything to do with us."⁷ This is probably the main difference between "new" and "old" professionals. Old professionals were insular. They were not necessarily corrupt or inefficient or technologically unsophisticated. They were adequately trained in the law of arrest, the penal code, interrogation tactics, and the fine points of when and how to apply a truncheon, and they had memorized their departments' rulebooks to prepare for promotional examinations. As trained technicians, they saw little advantage in seeking input or direction from the lay community. Like traditional firefighters, who are skilled in putting fires out rather than educating citizens to prevent fires, they were interested in solving, not preventing, crime. Unlike the tough and streetwise Davis, they also kept their distance from the street cop, regarding their own attainment of rank as the best evidence that they had a lock on whatever it took to run their departments.

The old guard didn't want to hear from the community. They told us they were professionals and that they didn't want to have anything to do with us.

Community policing involves not only sympathetic listening but the creation of opportunities to listen. This is a big step for most police forces, because what lay persons have to say may not be entirely flattering. Nevertheless, where community policing has been introduced, the police have learned that they must be prepared to listen, even if what they hear is unpleasant. Actually, when Neighborhood Watch and similar community programs are established, there rarely is serious unpleasantness, since the police and the citizens who participate generally are interested in fostering dialogue rather than hostility.

But who are these citizens? Of what "community" are they representative? As Wesley Skogan has cautioned, "advocates of Community Policing need to spell out clearly just how the police can come to know what a neighborhood wants in the way of order."⁸ The idea of community implies a commonality of interests, traditions, identities, values, and expectations. As we have suggested, these criteria may not be met in demographically complex and differentiated areas. Skogan reports that "in the outcomes of the Community Policing projects in Houston—there was a clear tendency for whites and homeowners (a surrogate measure of class) to enjoy the benefits of the programs, and for blacks and renters to be unaffected by them."[9] Community members who feel most comfortable with police—and with whom the police feel most comfortable—are the ones who enjoy stability of residence, jobs, businesses, and professions.

Whatever the limitations about assumptions of community, one compelling fact stands out in its favor in the policing context. Whenever surveys of ordinary people—of all races and political inclinations—are conducted, it turns out that most people (not most criminals, who go unpolled) prefer a police presence. Instead of despising the sight of police, people who work, ride public transportation, and send their children to school feel safer in the presence of police. Foot cops, who are the most approachable of police, are the most popular of all.[10]

The New York plan for community policing

In 1990 New York City, under [then-]Commissioner Lee P. Brown, envisioned a major expansion of community-oriented policing. Announced by [then-]Mayor David Dinkins, the "plan . . . maps out a strategy for weaving the fabric of community policing into our neighborhoods."[11] The plan called for hiring new officers to raise the patrol strength of the New York Police Department (NYPD), many of whom would be assigned to the Community Officer Patrol Program. Here, foot patrol officers would be given flexibility to develop contacts with residents and community groups in order to solve problems that result in crime, rather than merely responding to calls for service.

This implementation of community-oriented policing points to two of its other tightly wound features. One is decentralization of command; the other is problem-oriented policing. Although police operations may be geographically decentralized into local precincts or station houses, local tactics, assignments, priorities, shifts, and so forth are usually centrally established. By contrast, community policing assumes that policing problems and priorities vary from neighborhood to neighborhood. To accomplish this flexibility, local commanders must be given greater freedom and authority to respond to local conditions. Santa Ana, for example, was divided into four areas, where teams of police and associated community service officers would be assigned for substantial time periods, two or more years. The first step in community-policing reform in Adelaide, Australia, was a redrawing of subdivisional boundaries to make them coincide with smaller, more organic communities. In New York City entire precincts are being organized around community-oriented policing. Indeed, in response to suggestions by the Christopher Commission [Independent Commission on the Los Angeles Police Department], LAPD's [former Chief of Police] Daryl Gates announced shortly before the 1992 riot that a community-based policing experiment would soon begin in six of the city's eighteen police districts. The extent to which this LAPD program would involve decentralization and grassroots decision-making, however, was put in doubt by Chief Gates's decision to place it under his own close personal supervision.[12]

Para-police

Civilianizing the police force—hiring civilians to do the jobs cops formerly did so as to free patrol officers to work the streets—is a general

trend in policing. Years ago, fully qualified officers, known as *sworn* police, since they had qualified to take the oath of office, undertook virtually every job in the department, from detective to dispatcher. Yet by
1973 the National Advisory Commission on Criminal Justice Standards
and Goals, surveying forty-one metropolitan police departments, found
an average of 16 percent civilians to 84 percent sworn. Today, urban police departments rarely, if ever, employ sworn police to serve as dispatch-
ers and may employ as many as 40 percent civilians, although the average is about two sworn officers to every civilian.[13]

Civilianization of policing is thus quite acceptable. The controversial
issue is how deeply into the policing function to civilianize, an issue that
splits police chiefs who say they are otherwise supporters of community-
oriented policing and that sometimes raises the anxiety and the bitter opposition of police unions.

Santa Ana, California, a department in which community-oriented
policing was pioneered by Chief Raymond Davis in the 1970s and 1980s,
introduced a highly developed para-policing program—a concept modeled on the paramedic or paralegal—as an intrinsic aspect of community-
oriented policing.[14] In this vision, para-police were trained semiprofes-
sionals who performed important, but more routine, preliminary or
peripheral police tasks, usually connected with service to citizens. The
para-cops, who were usually female, were not responsible for investigating criminal activities or for apprehending and arresting those suspected
of crime. The central feature of the police role, the capacity to use force,
was thus not assigned to the para-police, who wore uniforms but carried
neither batons nor guns. (The SAPD had originally considered outfitting
para-police in blue blazers to distinguish them from sworn police officers
but found, after a brief experiment with blazers, that the blue uniform
signaled the only sort of authority citizens were willing to accept.)

The SAPD believed that nine para-police could be hired at the cost of
five sworn officers and could offer equally good *service*. In fact, many of
the para-police turned out to be better qualified because they could en-
rich *communication* with the sizable Spanish-speaking population of Santa
Ana. Investigation of major crimes involves a lot of talking—to the victim
as well as to neighbors, relatives, and friends. If you can't speak the language of the neighborhood, you can't investigate the crime. How can police investigate a homicide of a Salvadoran or Vietnamese victim if no
cops can speak the language of the victim?

Whenever surveys of ordinary people—of all races
and political inclinations—are conducted, it turns
out that most people (not most criminals, who go
unpolled) prefer a police presence.

As might be expected, para-police in Santa Ana participated in such
commonplace community-oriented policing tasks as organizing and
monitoring neighborhood watch groups and presenting crime prevention seminars, usually alongside sworn officers so as to signal the SAPD's
commitment to community policing. But they also marked abandoned
vehicles and had them towed; took reports of crimes, burglaries, and
rapes that had occurred earlier; and recontacted crime victims. This was

not so much to solve the crime—often beyond anyone's ability—but to support crime victims emotionally, a responsibility to which the SAPD assigned a high priority. Para-police also, as it happened, turned out to be unusually effective traffic investigators. Patrol cops generally disdain traffic accident investigations, especially the paperwork accompanying "fender benders." But for the para-police, their knowledge of the necessary paperwork for traffic accident investigations evidenced *their* professional expertise. As a result, para-police took accident investigations and reports seriously and tended to be more empathetic with, and helpful to, those involved. The Chief shrewdly realized that, for the average working stiff, the seemingly minor fender bender might be the most important and traumatic event of the month. Eventually, para-police were even successfully assigned to patrol cars, alone, equipped only with a radio. When they saw signs of trouble suggesting that force or arrest was needed, they would call one or more sworn cops.

Para-police present the policing world with a dilemma: Since they are fundamentally a cost-cutting measure, their pay needs to be much lower—about half—than that of sworn officers. But the better they perform, and as they are also assigned to midnight and weekend shifts, the more they threaten the pay scales and job security of sworn police. Police unions are accordingly wary of the whole idea of para-police. Cops are not *independent* and highly paid professionals, like doctors and lawyers, and so they see para-police not as heighteners of their status and professionalism but as potential union-busters. Top police managers, on the other hand, are more interested, since para-cops save costs and perform some tasks even better than sworn cops. One way some police departments have moved to resolve the dilemma is to pay para-police salaries approaching those of sworn police, but to exclude them from the generous pension and similar benefits that sworn cops enjoy.

Problem-oriented policing

"Problem-oriented policing," advocated by Herman Goldstein, a University of Wisconsin law professor,[15] is frequently identified with community-oriented policing, and for good reason. Both strategies stand in opposition to incident-driven policing. Traditionally, patrol police are deployed to respond to emergency calls for service. The dominant objectives of police patrol are to arrive quickly, stabilize the situation, and return to service— which means being available to answer another call. Inevitably, the response of most police officers is hasty and superficial. They may be critically important to minimize damage, but they have little time for or interest in responding to the underlying situation. Incident-driven patrol officers are usually well aware of their own limitations.

Consequently, according to Goldstein, incident-driven policing wastes time and impact. Police are neither solving problems nor preventing crime. By concentrating on incidents, the police lose control of their own resources and their own effectiveness. Most of their human resources are tied down by a commitment that diverts them from addressing the underlying crime and disorder problems of modern communities.

The solution, according to Goldstein, is for the police to become problem-oriented rather than incident-oriented. As in community-oriented policing, the emphasis is on police *pro*activity rather than *re*activity. Police are advised to diagnose longer-term solutions to recurrent crime and disorder problems and to mobilize community and municipal resources to implement them. Like community-oriented policing, problem-oriented policing envisions an altered, and a more analytical and humanistic, police role. Police must be able to perceive underlying problems, evaluate the feasibility and costliness of alternatives, work with others to design and implement solutions, vigorously advocate the adoption of necessary programs, monitor the results of cooperative efforts, and redirect them if necessary. The objective of policing doesn't change. It is still the enhancement of public safety and order. What changes is the way resources are allocated to meet the goal, so that police can now make a difference.

Police are advised to diagnose longer-term solutions to recurrent crime and disorder problems and to mobilize community and municipal resources to implement them.

Problem-oriented policing has been tried in several police departments. In one of the earliest examples offered by Goldstein, police in Madison, Wisconsin, were constantly summoned to the downtown shopping mall to deal with people who were behaving bizarrely and disruptively. Press reports put the number involved at one thousand and portrayed the mall as a haven for vagrants and street people. Not surprisingly, the public began to avoid the mall, and business suffered. When the police studied the problem over a period of time, they discovered that only thirteen individuals were responsible; that all had been under psychological supervision; and that they behaved strangely only when they failed to take their medication. The police began to work with mental health authorities, who developed a tighter supervision system for those people. The problem in the mall soon vanished, business returned, and the police were free to turn to other matters.[16]

As in community-oriented policing, problem-oriented policing should, above all, advocate a change in the philosophy of policing. The organization must be more flexible and willing to adapt to changing needs. The police officer, in turn, is required to be more of a generalist, more humanistic, more in tune with the underlying needs, problems, and resources of the areas being policed. Such an orientation is far less likely to generate police violence than traditional patrol policing, with which the familiar culture of policing is associated.

Two hurdles of community- and problem-oriented policing can be especially difficult. One is clarifying the definition of disorder and of fitting responses to it. The other is the distance between management cop philosophy and street cop behavior.

Disorder, as the political scientist Wesley Skogan has observed, encompasses various kinds of social and physical disarray.[17] It incorporates everything from junk and trash in vacant lots to boarded-up homes, broken windows, stripped and abandoned cars, graffiti, and animal waste in streets. It can also include such criminal activities as public drinking, drug selling, gambling, and prostitution, along with such ambiguous legal categories as "loitering," "disturbing the peace," and "panhandling." The sort of physical disarray and behavioral impropriety conveyed by the term "disorder," combined with a mandate to police to rid the community of it, can be interpreted as an invitation to police to "crack down," to become "badge-heavy," to "kick ass and take names." Indeed, one of the most vexing problems in controlling police violence is that it is so strongly supported in the most disorderly neighborhoods. In conveying an understanding that policing involves a range of problems and not just crime; that problems require analysis and differentiated responses; and that police are limited in their capacity to address these problems and need to involve the community, it would be paradoxical if police were to resort to the kind of aggressive patrolling that community-oriented and problem-oriented policing were supposed to eliminate, and that are often a prelude to violence.

These orientations toward policing are just that, orientations rather than orders, perspectives rather than prescriptions. They offer ways of looking at the world of policing, opportunities to step back and to reconstitute. As Herman Goldstein observes regarding problem-oriented policing:

> I have seen elaborate but totally unrealistic schedules for "full implementation" that seem more appropriate to a military exercise than to implementing a complex, necessarily long-term plan for organizational change requiring a radical change in the way in which employees view their job and carry it out.[18]

Overcoming street cop resistance

It takes a considerable amount of thinking to effect meaningful police reform efforts. Too often, "reform" consists of hiring a new and progressive chief without any provision for ensuring that an administration's lofty ideals are understood and implemented at the street level. Hardboiled street cops are led by their work to value order and stability. Hence, they often react to innovations in policing by deriding them as pointless and unworkable intrusions into the true and eternal work of the cop—the role they were recruited into and learned when they joined the department. Their representatives, the heads of police unions, often throw roadblocks in the path of reform as well. Unions will surely oppose civilian review, and they are inclined to be suspicious of accountability to anyone other than a known superior. If community-oriented and problem-oriented policing demand organizational flexibility, chiefs may find that changes—as, for example, in shifts and assignments—will be resisted in increasingly popular "meet and confer" bargaining sessions with police unions.

There are two ways to deal with line police officers' resistance to change. One way is to force change on officers from the top; to press down on cops and *compel* them to go along with change. Once this process is started, however, it cannot be stopped. Like a hand moved off the lid of a jack-in-the-box, any relaxation in pressure is sure to activate a counterreaction that will, to mix metaphors, swing the pendulum of change back far beyond the point where it had been when reform efforts started. Reform by intimidation from the top produces great tensions and lasts in police agencies only as long as the administrations of the intimidating chiefs who initiate it. Worse, it is our experience that street cops take every opportunity and use considerable ingenuity to undermine reform-by-intimidation even while such chiefs are in office.

More lasting and tension-free changes result from *enlisting* officers in reform efforts. The highest-ranking police officials in Oakland, Dade County [Florida], and New York were absolutely committed to reform, but the actual shapes of the reforms were developed far down the organizational chain by good street cops who had been asked to diagnose a problem and then empowered to fit to it their definitions of *good policing*. The officers in all of these projects embraced their tasks so vigorously, we are convinced, because the process in which they participated—*peer establishment of standards and development of means of assessing the extent to which they have been attained*—more closely approximated professionalism than anything they had previously experienced in their police careers.

Such an orientation is far less likely to generate police violence than traditional patrol policing, with which the familiar culture of policing is associated.

In this sense, introducing meaningful reforms that *last* is a far greater challenge to those at the top of police departments than to those at the bottom. If a police department is to be truly *professionalized*, authority and responsibility must be decentralized. The brass must surrender some of their prerogatives and must empower those further down the line to define the challenges of their work and to develop means of addressing them. Regardless of their high-toned rhetoric and claimed commitment to police professionalism, community-oriented policing, and the like, many top police officials are unwilling to do this. As a consequence, the reality of community-oriented policing seen through the windshields of police patrol cars sometimes is very different from that described in the glowing terms of police departments' brochures and brag-sheets or by distant police chiefs who are unwilling to delegate any authority to the street cops and supervisors closest to communities and their problems. When that happens, the polarization of what Elizabeth Reuss-Ianni called the two cultures of policing—management cops and street cops[19]—grows. An officer in a police department undergoing a highly publicized "conversion" to a community-oriented policing model told us:

> This is the usual horseshit. The chief tells everybody that we're community-oriented, but we still don't know what that means. The chief goes out and makes speeches about it, but when we ask the sergeant what we should say to people if they ask us about this, he tells us to keep in mind the department's rule that we're not allowed to criticize any department policy or official. I guess it would be critical to tell people we have no idea what the difference between community-oriented policing and what we used to do is, so we just smile and nod.[20]

The officer's point is well taken. We have seen many fads in policing over the years, and police chiefs are no less likely than any other officials to wrap themselves in trendy jargon at the same time that they keep their distance from real change.

Notes

1. For overviews of community policing, see Skolnick and David Bayley, *The New Blue Line: Police Innovation in Six American Cities* (New York: Free Press, 1986); Jerome H. Skolnick and David Bayley, *Community Policing: Issues and Practices Around the World* (Washington, DC: National Institute of Justice, 1988); and Wesley Skogan, *Disorder and Decline: Crime and the*

Spiral of Decay in American Neighborhoods (New York: Free Press, 1990).

2. Albert J. Reiss, Jr., *Policing a City's Central District: The Oakland Story* (Washington, DC: National Institute of Justice, 1985).

3. See George L. Kelling, Tony Pate, Duane Dieckman, and Charles E. Brown, *The Kansas City Preventive Patrol Experiment: Summary Report* (Washington, DC: Police Foundation, 1974); Police Foundation, *The Newark Foot Patrol Experiment* (Washington, DC, 1981); and William G. Spelman and Dale K. Brown, *Calling the Police: A Replication of the Kansas City Response Time Analysis* (Washington, DC: Police Executive Research Forum, 1981).

4. See, e.g., Spelman and Brown, *Calling the Police.*

5. See, e.g., Edward H. Kaplan, "Evaluating the Effectiveness of One Officer Versus Two Officer Patrol Units," *Journal of Criminal Justice*, 7 (Winter 1979):325-55.

6. Norwegian Official Reports, *The Role of the Police in the Society*, NOU 35 (Oslo: Universitetforlaget, 1981).

7. Skolnick and Bayley, *The New Blue Line*, pp. 20-21.

8. Skogan, *Disorder and Decline*, p. 167.

9. *Ibid.*

10. See, e.g., Police Foundation, *Newark Foot Patrol Experiment.*

11. *Criminal Justice Newsletter*, vol. 21, October 15, 1990.

12. Ted Rohrlich, "Gates' Community-Based Policing Plan OKd," *Los Angeles Times*, January 22, 1992.

13. Peter Strawbridge and Deirdre Strawbridge, *A Networking Guide to Recruitment, Selection and Probationary Training of Police Officers in Major Police Departments of the United States* (New York: John Jay College, 1990).

14. See Skolnick and Bayley, *The New Blue Line*, pp. 13-50.

15. See Herman Goldstein, "Improving Policing: A Problem-Oriented Approach," *Crime and Delinquency*, 25 (1979):236-58. *Problem-Oriented Policing* (New York: McGraw-Hill, 1990).

16. Goldstein, "Improving Policing."

17. Skogan, *Disorder and Decline*, esp. pp. 3-9.

18. Goldstein, *Problem-Oriented Policing*, p. 178.

19. Elizabeth Reuss-Ianni, *Two Cultures of Policing: Street Cops and Management Cops* (New Brunswick, NJ: Transaction Books, 1983).

20. Personal communication with James J. Fyfe, July 26, 1991.

5

Civilian Oversight Is Necessary to Prevent Police Brutality

Mary D. Powers

Mary D. Powers directs the work of Citizens Alert, Chicago's civilian oversight group, and the National Coalition on Police Accountability, a coalition of civilian review organizations.

Due to police excesses, civilian oversight boards are needed to review police misconduct. Powerless groups—minorities, the poor, and young people—are the usual victims of police brutality. Civilian oversight can empower these groups to fight back against police brutality. Citizens Alert, Chicago's civilian oversight board, is a successful example.

The need for police accountability is not new. Centuries ago the Roman writer Juvenal asked *"Quis custodiet ipsos custodes?"*—"Who is to guard the guardians themselves?" The question is as pertinent now as it was then.

Recurring incidents of excessive force, unnecessary shootings, racial harassment and the informal code of silence requiring officers to cover-up and deny irresponsible behavior by their colleagues are now familiar to the average citizen. Television flashes of the beating of Rodney King have seared the scene into the nation's memory. Former Los Angeles Police Chief Daryl Gates termed it an "aberration," but subsequent accounts of Detroit police [officers Larry Nevers and Walter Budzyn] beating Malice Green to death [in November 1992] contradicted this explanation. [The officers were found guilty of murder in November 1993—ed.]

More recently [1993], sworn testimony of police officers before the Mollen Commission [Commission to Investigate Allegations of Police Corruption and the Anti-Corruption Procedures of the New York City Police Department] investigating corruption in New York confirmed our worst suspicions. A "clean-cut" former patrolman admitted how, in four years of public service, he randomly had attacked people with his nightstick, flashlight, and/or lead-lined gloves in as many as 400 incidents. He described being nicknamed "the mechanic" by superiors acknowledging his skill in administering "tune-ups," a police term for beatings. When

Mary D. Powers, "Who Polices the Police?" *Christian Social Action*, November 1993. Reprinted with permission.

asked if those "tuned-up" were suspects, he replied, "No, I was just beating up people in general."

To comprehend how deeply ingrained this lack of accountability has become, one need only examine police reactions to a proposal by the mayor of New York for a civilian board to review complaints of misconduct. To demonstrate their anger, thousands of off-duty officers broke through police barricades to storm the steps of City Hall, damaged parked cars, and blocked traffic on the Brooklyn Bridge. Racially derogatory slogans were chanted and displayed on signs [by police] deriding their commander-in-chief, New York's first African-American mayor [David Dinkins].

Civilian review and control needed

This event provided a clear illustration of the urgent need for civilian review and control of police conduct. Who could trust such guardians of peace to monitor their own activities? Professor Tracey Maclin of Boston University School of Law described the violent overreaction as "outlaw behavior, which went uncontrolled" (*Viewpoint*, New York Newsday Editorials, October 7, 1992). "Police officers assigned to the area did nothing to restrain the unruly mob and no arrests were reported," he wrote.

Such flaunting of lawful authority gives the law-abiding citizen little reason to have confidence in or respect for those hired to serve and protect. This kind of disruptive police conduct raises a recurring question that the public is often reluctant to confront: Who controls the police?

Excessive force, unnecessary shootings, racial harassment and the informal code of silence . . . are now familiar to the average citizen.

Public trust and cooperation are essential for effective crime prevention. Many police departments are initiating new programs that necessitate exchange of information and forging new partnerships with the communities they serve. Community policing is the new order of the day, and never before has the need for citizen cooperation been so great. Cities across the country are immersed in spiraling crime, increased violence, mounting racial tensions aggravated by high rates of unemployment, ready access to drugs and weapons by persons of all ages, and everywhere an overburdened criminal justice system.

The first step into that criminal justice system is the initial interaction on the street between police and citizen. Public scrutiny should begin here. Taxpayers have not only a right, but a responsibility to see that such interactions are appropriate, lawful, and within the bounds of police department's policies and procedures.

Temptations to make quick arrests

More and more, when police are often outarmed by gangs and seven-year-olds act as lookouts for drug dealers, temptations to make quick arrests, demonstrate police authority, and resolve possibly volatile confrontations at the scene may take precedence over professional, thorough police work. Probable cause may be overlooked; due process may be ignored. For the unfortunate person unable to post bond or make bail, a speedy trial is highly unlikely, and any public defender assigned inevitably is overworked.

Thus, another addition is made to the courts, the jail, and the prison statistics, which are already soaring to unprecedented heights. Tax dollars desperately needed to alleviate hunger, homelessness, and infant mortality are diverted to unnecessary and sometimes unwarranted arrests, prosecution and incarceration.

Each unnecessary arrest, especially those unjustified by lack of criminal behavior, adds to the burden of the criminal justice system. Therefore, this first step is a key point for civilian scrutiny and oversight.

The first step into that criminal justice system is the initial interaction on the street between police and citizen. Public scrutiny should begin here.

Almost every instance of brutality is accompanied by an arrest. This way a citizen's injuries can be explained. A report may say that they are a result of the necessary force needed while the victim was "resisting arrest" or "obstructing justice." This is the key spot where the "code of silence" by fellow officers goes into play. The New York patrolman who admits to over 400 incidents of random attacks on citizens would usually have arrested, or at least taken into custody, 400 innocent persons for no apparent reason other than to fabricate an excuse lest they file complaints against him.

National statistics show that the usual victims of brutality are people of color, the poor, the young—people perceived by the police to be powerless. Because of being singled out so frequently, these communities lack confidence in any investigative mechanisms that assign police officers to investigate their colleagues' conduct. The low rates of verification and discipline resulting from such complaints are often interpreted as official indifference to abuse of African-American and Latino victims. Such lack of confidence is echoed in the broader community, as well. There are increasing demands for independent civilian review boards to investigate complaints and recommend discipline.

A community response—Citizens Alert

Long before the videotape of Rodney King's beating shocked viewers into a new awareness of the need for police accountability, Citizens Alert, in Chicago, was dealing with the issue. Founded in 1967, the non-profit watchdog group has the goal of more humane and effective law enforcement. It attempts to improve understanding and communication between police and community.

Using a five-pronged approach, volunteers assist victims of police abuse and serve as civil rights advocates, monitor police conduct and policies to assure greater accountability to the public, recommend policy changes that may result in more humane and/or effective law enforcement, build coalitions to involve other organizations in specific police issues, and maintain a growing national network of individuals and groups working on accountability issues.

Making citizens aware of their rights, helping victims to file complaints and providing an opportunity to do something about police harassment and abuse are major steps in alleviating the hopelessness of many victims. Citizens Alert involves neighborhood groups, social justice committees, progressive reform-minded police and the victims themselves in the struggle for community justice. Although an overall goal is to end police brutality, advocacy and empowerment for victims and their families is an ongoing commitment.

In 1989 a new dimension of police brutality became an issue in Chicago with reports of a white police commander of detectives systematically torturing (by electroshock, partial suffocation, Russian Roulette) over 70 African-American suspects during interrogation. In order to counteract the many legal maneuvers, dirty tricks, cover-ups, and constant resistance by the Fraternal Order of Police, Citizens Alert convened the broad-based Coalition to End Police Torture and Brutality.

After four years of community education, marches, rallies, media and letter writing campaigns, the Chicago Police Board fired the commander on February 10, 1993. This was an unprecedented firing of someone of that high rank for use of excessive force. The police board president credited Citizens Alert and the coalition with "keeping the case alive."

A national response after the King beating

Shortly after the Rodney King beating, the coalition, in cooperation with the National Interreligious Task Force on Criminal Justice, convened a national conference in Chicago. This resulted in the formation of the National Coalition on Police Accountability (N-COPA), an organization of religious, community and legal groups, and progressive law enforcement representatives working to hold police accountable to their communities through public education, community organizing, legislation, litigation, and the promotion of empowered civilian oversight.

Groups from across the country are represented and come together periodically to share successes and failures, develop strategies, and determine specific programs to address policy accountability issues. The first N-COPA newsletter will be published this year [1993].

None of these efforts would have been possible without consistent encouragement, resources, and cooperation from church sources, both local and national. Citizens Alert feels that it is truly a ministry of justice, and welcomes the opportunity to help develop similar projects.

As we recognize the wide discretion given to police, it is essential that we assume civilian responsibility for how that discretion is used or abused.

Nine years ago [in 1984] the International Association for Civilian Oversight of Law Enforcement (IACOLE) was established. Members from throughout the world—including the United States, Canada, Australia, Hong Kong, Ireland and South Africa—met in Cambridge, Massachusetts [in 1993] to share information and expertise on promotion of civilian oversight mechanisms. Their focus is primarily to represent established review boards, and many versions, weak and strong, were represented. (Citizens Alert is an associate member, as its focus is primarily on community-based efforts toward accountability.)

On local, national, and international levels, a strong movement is developing to require new accountability of law enforcement to the public. The focus has widened to include federal agencies, as well. The Immigration Law Enforcement Monitoring Project of the American Friends Service Committee is promoting legislation to require civilian oversight of the Immigration and Naturalization Service and US Border Patrol, whose abuses have been historic.

Every year dozens of cities establish review boards, while citizen groups multiply their efforts for accountability mechanisms. Progressive police administrators recognize the need and are becoming more cooperative. Consultants from Citizens Alert, N-COPA, and IACOLE are available and willing to provide information.

Vigilance to prevent abuses of power

"It would be a dangerous situation if our confidence in the men of our choice should silence our fears for the safety of our rights. . . . In questions of power, then, let no more be heard on confidence in man, but bind him down from mischief by the chains of the Constitution." Thomas Jefferson

These words spoken over two hundred years ago by one of the founders of the United States should alert us today to the need for eternal vigilance to prevent abuse of power. Police have broad discretion in their use of arrest, the degree of force they deem necessary and even in the use of firearms. It is necessary to recognize this discretion openly and monitor it carefully. Unchecked police power is the first step to totalitarian government.

In his book *Policing in a Free Society*, Professor Herman Goldstein of the University of Wisconsin, a former police administrator himself, speaks to the issue by explaining that police personnel have been viewed traditionally as performing a "ministerial function." He emphasizes that police have been assumed to be following precise legal mandates and applying them absolutely uniformly. On the contrary, police constantly must make choices and exercise wide discretion in juggling their multiple and sometimes conflicting responsibilities.

As we recognize the wide discretion given to police, it is essential that we assume civilian responsibility for how that discretion is used or abused. Too often in the traditional view of police as being the thin blue line that protects the law-abiding from the criminal, fear of crime and of becoming a victim easily leads to an acceptance that whatever a police officer does should not be challenged. The Constitution, however, specifically positions our rights to privacy, personal security, and human dignity as higher priorities than society's interest in catching criminals.

Whether racism, classism or homophobia by local police, *apartheid* governmental policies, or Central American armies of repression, the reactions are the same: resistance, rebellion, or hopelessness. People must become aware that no matter whose rights are abused by whatever police agency in the world, the rights of all of us are affected. By joining together in community to redirect and challenge the police forces of the world, we are protecting our rights and promoting a just peace.

6

A Police Corps Will Reduce Crime Rates and Improve Police-Community Relations

John Carlisle

John Carlisle is a policy analyst who specializes in crime issues at the Free Congress Research and Education Foundation, a political action committee. He has written several articles for Policy Insights, *a publication of the Free Congress Foundation, including "Volunteer Cops: The New Minutemen."*

Because crime rates are increasing faster than the number of police in American cities, street cops and tough laws are needed to rebuild law and order. The Police Corps plan will provide scholarships to college students who volunteer four years of service to local police forces, providing an immediate increase in the number of police on patrol. Graduates of the Police Corps will include minorities and enthusiastic volunteers who can change the "police culture" that fosters brutality and corruption.

In the United States today, a crime is committed every two seconds. This includes:

- a murder every 24 minutes
- a rape every 6 minutes
- a robbery every 55 seconds
- an aggravated assault every 33 seconds
- a motor vehicle theft every 20 seconds
- a burglary every 10 seconds

Since 1957, the number of reported violent crimes in the U.S. has soared 436 percent so that by 1988, there occurred 20,675 murders, 92,486 rapes, 542,968 robberies, and 910,092 assaults. On average today, 464 Americans are murdered every week.

The question can be fairly asked, "Why can't we stop crime?" After all, it isn't as if we haven't tried. For the past two decades, politicians from presidents to mayors have devoted a substantial amount of their rhetoric to decrying lawlessness and calling for more law and order. In response to the almost annual declarations of war on crime, the courts have tough-

John Carlisle, "Crime, Cops, and Civil Peace," *Essays on Our Times*, vol. 13, November 1991. Reprinted by permission of the Free Congress Research and Education Foundation.

ened sentences and restricted criminal rights while federal and state governments have invested billions of dollars in new prisons and billions more in sweeping social programs that supposedly deal with the root causes of crime. But all to no avail.

Crime overwhelms police

A major reason for this failure is the lack of proper law enforcement where it really counts—on the streets. Since 1957, the number of policemen has increased from 1.6 per thousand people to 2.6 per thousand. At first glance, this near doubling of the nation's 20,000 police departments suggests that law enforcement has reasonably kept up with the upsurge in crime—until one takes into account that the crime rate increased ten times over in the same period. Thus, what is truly striking is that the increase in policemen has been consistently overwhelmed by the inflation in crime.

In 1951, there were 3 police officers for every felony. Today, there are 3 felonies for every officer. In 1951, Buffalo, New York, had 1,229 officers to handle 361 violent crimes. But by 1988, the number of violent crimes jumped to 3,555 while the police force shrunk to 970. That is a felony-to-cop ratio of nearly 4 to 1. New York City's history is similar. In 1951, the city's 19,000 police officers had to contend with 244 homicides and 7,000 robberies. In 1988, the force of 27,000 had to contend with 1,800 murders and 80,000 robberies—a ratio of more than 3 to 1.

This shocking discrepancy between law enforcement officers and the number of violent crimes holds true for virtually every major city. To take but a few examples:

- In Boston, the crime-to-cop ratio is 6 to 1
- Atlanta, 10 to 1
- Cleveland, 4 to 1
- Chicago, 5 to 1
- Newark, 8 to 1
- Miami, 11 to 1
- Tampa, 12 to 1
- Los Angeles, 9 to 1
- Oakland, 11 to 1

The discrepancy widens even further in the poorer, predominantly black cities. In East St. Louis, Illinois, there are 26.7 crimes per officer. In Compton, California, the ratio is almost 28 felonies to 1.

In short, the United States is devoting merely *one ninth* the police power of thirty-five years ago to today's violent crime epidemic. As to be expected, the result is nothing short of a catastrophe. As many as one third of 911 calls go unanswered by many police departments due to sheer lack of manpower.

Years ago, homicides had a 90 percent clearance rate. A clearance rate is the rate at which police make an arrest for a crime. But today, the percentage of crime cleared or leading to arrest has drastically fallen. The homicide clearance rate is now only 70 percent. That is, police do not make an arrest for 30 percent of reported homicides. This is a frightening figure indeed. Since more than 20,000 murders occur every year, that means almost 7,000 murders reported to the police go unsolved.

The figures get worse when all violent crime is included. In many areas of the nation, the clearance rate for violent crime is less than 50 percent. A good example is Massachusetts. In 1960, before the crime wave, 71 percent of all violent crimes committed in Massachusetts led to an arrest. By 1982, that figure had fallen to less than 44 percent.

The disturbing gap between the number of crimes and cops becomes downright shocking when it is taken into account that many arrests require more than one officer. For instance, a drug arrest alone requires five officers: two undercover, two uniformed, and one to handle the paperwork. And to make matters worse, the court requires that a suspect be arrested, booked, and into jail within a three-hour period. The police simply can't keep up.

It is clear that bold steps must be taken to restore the nation's overburdened police forces. Unfortunately, such clarion calls to strengthen police in their desperate war against lawlessness are hardly new. One need only recall Nixon's law and order platform culminating in a federal program of assistance to state and local police forces. But despite all the rhetoric, declarations of war, hearings, commissions, and public indignation, the nation's 20,000 police departments continue to be plagued by a lack of resources and manpower. And after so many years of tough talk but little results, the public has become increasingly apathetic and cynical about government's—and their own—ability to reclaim their streets and neighborhoods from hoodlums.

Reinforcing the ranks

Now, however, there is an innovative and sweeping proposal [passed by] Congress [in Summer 1994] that *will* have a major impact on law enforcement. It is a proposal that costs relatively little but whose results would be immediately seen in virtually every American city—especially those hit hardest by crime. The proposal is called the Police Corps.

Police Corps is the brainchild of Adam Walinsky, New York lawyer and former aide to the late Senator Robert Kennedy. Mr. Walinsky came up with the idea more than a decade ago and has been doggedly lobbying politicians, police chiefs, and law school deans ever since. Police Corps is simply an ROTC [Reserve Officers' Training Corps] program for the police. It would offer college students scholarships of up to $10,000 per year in exchange for a four-year stint in a police force.

The purpose: to inject thousands of police officers into the streets of battered cities and restore a long-lost sense of domestic peace for millions of American citizens. There are many reasons for crime—economic, social, moral—and thus a number of solutions. But, as Mr. Walinsky points out, "no other measure can hope to be effective unless we immediately strengthen our police forces on a scale dramatically greater than any thus far proposed."

The importance of the street cop

For the average citizen, the police—that is, the officers on the street—are their only tangible connection with law and order. Because of the rapid spread of crime, misguided budget priorities, and poor management decisions, the officer on the beat has retreated from battered neighborhoods. Walinsky argues: "The cops used to be there when you needed them. . . . Today, they operate from a station house or from squad cars—like Vietnam, doing sporadic battle but not really protecting hamlets."

Not surprisingly, many Americans, especially the inner-city poor, feel

abandoned by the system. The withdrawal of the police effectively trans-
ferred power from the forces of justice to the criminals. As a result, the
brutal manners, attitudes, and tactics of the ruling gangsters set the standards. The decent people, those who wanted to do good, go to school, get
a decent job, raise a family, and do all the other things our Constitution
supposedly guarantees, find themselves in a situation where they must
tolerate the gangsters' ethics or, worse, practice them.

This is not law enforcement; this is moral abdication. Good police
work means taking crime head-on, not tacitly giving it the go-ahead. And
that means spending time in a community, getting to know the residents,
establishing contacts, and building reliable communication networks.
Only by becoming a part of the community can a police officer fight the
ills of the community. A patrolman who knows his "constituents" very
often knows what to expect, that is, when a crime is to take place on his
turf. If not able to prevent a crime, his neighborhood contacts can enable
him to move swiftly against suspects.

---

*What is truly striking is that the increase in police-
men has been consistently overwhelmed by the inflation in crime.*

The most insulting thing the criminal element can do to the forces of
law and order is to openly flaunt that order. Many urban areas are characterized by open-air drug markets, daytime shootings occurring on an almost regular schedule, and worst of all a general disregard among criminals and noncriminals alike for the police as nothing better than ordinary
bystanders. For the criminal justice system to work, it has to have the
faith of the people. Such faith is nonexistent among millions of Americans.

The war against crime demands that the frontline be reinforced.
Building more prisons, adding more courts, and hiring more prosecutors
are all necessary. But if the average officer continues to work in a situation where he has to deal with an average of 3 felonies or as many as 20
in the worst areas, then that war will only yield mixed results at best.

Civic order can only be rebuilt if the nation's overburdened police
forces are reinforced. If gangsters, sadly to say, are going to become prominent fixtures in many cities, then their visibility and influence must be
matched and if possible more than matched by the representatives of law
and order. If hoodlums are going to menace the streets, we must at least
make it so that they can't practice their lawless trade so easily. All police
departments should be able to do on a regular basis what Charleston,
South Carolina, police did when they disrupted open-air drug markets
with periodic sweeps. Likewise, it should be possible for police to do what
desperate Washington, D.C., residents did when they disrupted open-air
drug markets by photographing, observing, and subtly threatening dealers. In other words, we must make it possible for the police to maintain a
presence. Where there is a lot of crime, police need a lot of manpower.

The policeman as deterrent

There is evidence that "saturating" high-crime areas with patrolmen can
have a major impact on the level of criminal activity. In 1954, the New

York City Police Department conducted an experiment called "Operation 25." For a four-month period, the number of officers in a high-crime area of Manhattan was doubled. The result: muggings fell from 69 to 7, auto thefts from 78 to 24, and assaults from 185 to 132. The one significant exception was murder, which increased from 6 in the previous four-month period to 8 during the period of heightened police protection. A possible explanation for the unaffected homicide rate is that many murders take place in private and are not as likely to be deterred by an officer on the street.

Increasing police presence deters crime because it increases the certainty of punishment. Herein lies the chief argument on behalf of focusing resources on the street cop instead of solely relying on tougher laws and more prisons. The average criminal in a low-income neighborhood tends to have a short-term mentality. Since he doesn't have much of a future, he never thinks about it. What he does think about is how he can find some "action"—to get money for drugs, food, clothes, or entertainment. He seeks instant gratification. By itself, a stiff penalty for his actions is just too distant a prospect to seriously affect his calculations of profit and loss. His only inhibition is the level of *immediate* risk attending a prospective crime. In other words, will he get caught? Unfortunately, the answer to that question is almost always no. A study estimated that the probability of a typical youth gang member's being arrested for a single offense is .04 percent, and .02 percent if he is very skillful. Hence, tough laws only have reality if the criminal knows he is running a very serious risk of being arrested.

How Police Corps works

Police Corps would give those tough laws reality. Under the current plan's provisions, 25,000 college students would be awarded scholarships of up to $40,000 to cover their educational costs. Within four years of adoption, the full complement of 100,000 Police Corps graduates would be working in police departments all over the nation. This represents a 20 percent increase in the current cadre of 488,000 police officers. Because virtually all the Police Corps graduates would be placed on the streets, the number of frontline patrolmen working the beat would jump by 40 percent. In areas of exceptionally high crime, the number of street patrolmen would double.

The distribution of graduates would depend on the population of a participating state, the number of Police Corps students in that state, and the local preferences of the graduates. To give some idea of Police Corps' dramatic impact, a New York reporter estimated that New York City would get an additional 7,000 personnel for its 27,000-man force.

Organizationally, Police Corps is modelled on the Marine Platoon Leaders Course. To begin with, applicants must meet the standards of the state and local police forces to which they will be assigned. Upon selection, students would choose the major and classes of their choice like ROTC students. They would not, however, be required to take any law-enforcement classes. In the summer after their junior year, the students would take an intensive eight-week training course at one of three federally planned Federal Law Enforcement training centers. Upon graduation, the prospective officer would take another eight-week course after which he would enter a police force within his state of residence. Local departments have the option of giving additional training to the graduates. Students would have the right to choose, albeit with some restrictions, the local police forces with which to do their four years of service. If the student fails to complete his education, the federal training program, or his four-year term of service, he will have to repay the entire loan plus interest to the government.

Civic order can only be rebuilt if the nation's over-burdened police forces are reinforced.

The program would be administered by an Office of the Police Corps within the Department of Justice. Its head, the Director, is to be appointed by the President and approved by the Senate. It is up to the individual states to decide if they want to participate in the program. If they choose to participate, the states must meet certain standards set forth by the Director of the Police Corps. Among the standards is that no more than 10 percent of graduates must be assigned to the State Police, that they be assigned to areas of greatest need, and in areas near the graduates' home or areas which they specifically request. Furthermore, graduates are to be placed, as much as possible, on community and preventive patrol.

In the first five years of the program, 10 percent of the applicants may have previous law enforcement experience. After the fifth year, however, no applicant with such experience would be eligible. Likewise, college juniors and seniors would be eligible in the early years to get the program started.

As far as federal programs go, Police Corps is a bargain. During its first year of operation, Police Corps would cost about $100 million. The total cost is projected to run to $1.4 billion once the full 100,000 students are on scholarship. Unlike many other multi-billion-dollar federal boondoggles, the investment in Police Corps will yield quick and decisive results in the form of heightened police protection, increased public confidence in the law-enforcement system, and a whole new generation of young Americans dedicated to national service.

Objections

Although the broadest possible bipartisan coalition has lined up behind Police Corps, there are a number of concerns raised which should be addressed. One is that Police Corps graduates would not be used as additions to the police force but rather as replacements. In this scenario, the federal government would inadvertently assume the local budgetary responsibilities without getting a concomitant increase in the number of law-enforcement officers. However, to prevent that, the Police Corps legislation has stipulated that no graduates be assigned to a department whose size has fallen by more than 5 percent since June 21, 1989.

The only worry expressed by police unions—who are otherwise very enthusiastic—is that Police Corps graduates might be used to subvert union agreements on wages and benefits. But this will pose no problem because Police Corps graduates are to be paid the same salaries as regular unionized personnel. This in turn led to concerns that many cash-strapped cities would not be able to afford a large influx of new patrolmen. However, Police Corps officers would not receive the expensive pension benefits of union cops. As a result, they will on average run the city only 70 percent of the normal cost for supporting an officer.

Other concerns expressed by some members of the law-enforcement community includes charges of elitism. College graduates are only interested, the argument goes, in a four-year stint to pay their education. As soon as their term of service is over, they will move on to their respective careers. In the meantime, resources that should be given to career officers are instead going to "freeloading" college students. However, elitism is probably the least of the problems with Police Corps. First of all, regular officers do not sign up for a given period of service. They can resign whenever they want. In fact, one-third resign after three years of service. It's also hard to believe that the presence of "elitist" college graduates in the ranks will cause animosity in the squad room. There are plenty of other units within the police forces of a far more elitist character, such as SWAT teams, anti-terrorist units, and narcotics squads.

The claim that resources can be better used to further the education of existing officers has to be looked at from the perspective of the crisis on American streets—a crisis requiring a swift response. And that response has to be to get as many new cops on the streets as possible. Whatever its other merits, increasing education funding for existing officers will not accomplish that task.

This is not to say that career officers are being ignored by the Police Corps legislation. Besides protecting police benefits and salaries, there are also provisions to increase education funding for police by $30 million. In addition, there is another provision which would give the same Police Corps scholarships to the children of officers killed in the line of duty without the four-year service requirement.

The combination of enthusiasm and advanced education can only serve to upgrade the quality of local police forces.

If anything, the infusion of new blood into the ranks of career officers can only be a boon to the physical and moral resources of a department. In the last several years, law-enforcement officials have been distressed by the inability to attract quality recruits. According to the director for testing, New York's Civil Service Test, required for all prospective officers, could be passed by a "functional illiterate." Philadelphia's police commissioner managed to "beef up" standards by requiring that new recruits have high school diplomas. [former] Washington, D.C., police chief Isaac Fulwood said that the District added funding for 300 new officers but could not find enough applicants. And the city of Miami had to fire a large part of its force for incompetence. The situation for minority recruits is even worse. After years of strenuous efforts and changes in admissions criteria, the number of quality black policemen is still extremely low. On a recent sergeant's test in New York City, only 2 percent of the black officers taking the test passed.

Enthusiastic college students are the answer to this woeful state of affairs. A Department of Justice survey found that 40 percent of college students would be likely to enter the program, including 45 percent of black students. In another survey, 88 percent of all police chiefs said they would use Police Corps graduates. This should come as no surprise since 80 percent said they were suffering a shortage. Many chiefs requested that they "send 'em next week."

The combination of enthusiasm and advanced education can only serve to upgrade the quality of local police forces. Young officers tend to be more vigorous and idealistic. It is noteworthy that officers with less than three years of experience make 30 percent of all arrests. Also, a good argument has been made that the idealism of Police Corps graduates will invigorate the cynical and alienating atmosphere of many squad rooms. This could counter the depressing police subculture which breeds burnout, corruption, and brutality among some veterans. The incident in Los Angeles where police beat an unarmed motorist [Rodney King] shows the urgency in breaking down this dangerous mentality.

Granted that many Police Corps recruits will leave after four years of service, it still can't be denied that a significant number will remain to make law enforcement a career. Through this program, the nation's police forces can be assured that a dedicated cadre of college graduates will be entering their ranks on an annual basis.

In a sense, Police Corps merely restores the balance that federal student loans inadvertently upset. Thirty years ago, only one-third of the top fifth of high school graduating classes entered college. From the remainder came the military's NCOs and cops. With the widespread availability of federal student loans, that source of police recruitment dried up. Police Corps seeks to make law enforcement attractive again for bright, ambitious young people.

Another dividend law enforcement will reap from Police Corps is a broader base of public support. Every year, thousands of college graduates will finish their police service and enter their chosen professions. These Police Corps veterans would form a natural constituency for law enforcement. James Fyfe, American University professor and former police officer, stated in congressional testimony that the lack of such a constituency, especially among policymakers and legislators, is a shame and only hurts the police. American government is replete with examples of former military men who used their service experience in formulating policy. However, there are few examples of former police officers going into government and exercising a similar influence.

Our recent successes in international policy are due in no small part to the military experience of top leaders. Now, with domestic policy, and crime in particular, assuming a more prominent role in American politics, it is urgent that we start building a cadre of ex-law-enforcement officials within government. If an effective crime-fighting strategy is to be devised, it is critical that elected officials and other policymakers have the requisite experience. Police Corps is a major step in that direction.

7

Inner-City Crime
Is a Worse Problem
than Police Brutality

William Tucker

William Tucker is the author of Vigilante: The Backlash Against Crime in America *and* Progress and Privilege.

Police officers are often unjustly charged with brutality. Police brutality is not the biggest problem that faces American society; crime among minority juveniles in the inner city is a worse problem. The problems of the inner cities—drugs, guns, and the disintegration of families—are overwhelming the order-maintenance efforts of police. Police reform efforts—such as civilian review boards, which invite frivolous complaints against police—disarm the police in their war on crime. Even if police adopt community policing, inner-city residents will see it as an intrusion.

Item: On July 20, 1992, Sergeant Peter Viola and four other New York City police officers were summoned to the home of Annie Dodds, a politically prominent black woman in Brooklyn, to settle a domestic dispute. It was one of those routinely dangerous, noncriminal confrontations that the police have learned to abhor.

Mrs. Dodds's two sons, Harold Dodds, 34, and Tyrese Daniels, 28, were engaged in a violent argument. Although the police could not then know it, both brothers had extensive criminal records. Daniels in particular had been charged several times with assaulting police officers.

As the five cops worked patiently to soothe tempers, Daniels suddenly turned on his brother and hit him over the head with a metal pipe he had been brandishing. In the ensuing melee, all five cops were injured, one suffering a fractured shoulder. Mrs. Dodds also suffered a few scratches. Nevertheless, she went to the Brooklyn district attorney, Charles Hynes, and complained of Sergeant Viola's behavior. Viola was subsequently charged with felonious assault and is now [as of late 1992] awaiting trial.

Item: In January 1992, Scott Baldwin, a 210-pound running back at the University of Nebraska, underwent a "psychotic episode," jumping out of a friend's car and running naked through the streets of Omaha. Coming across a woman walking her dog, Baldwin smashed her head into a parked car, nearly killing her. He was charged with assault, but acquitted by reason of insanity.

The coach of the Nebraska football team, Tom Osborne, then took Baldwin into his home for several months. But on September 5, the evening of Nebraska's first game of the season, Baldwin again turned up in Omaha, this time trying to break through the glass door of a stranger's apartment. Two female police officers were dispatched to the scene. When they tried to handcuff Baldwin, he wrestled one to the ground and attempted to grab her gun. The other officer drew her gun, held it to Baldwin's head, and threatened him. When Baldwin kept fighting, she lowered the gun and shot him in the ribs, paralyzing him for life.

State Senator Ernie Chambers of Omaha, Nebraska's only black legislator, blamed the police for sending two women to the scene and called the shooting "avoidable and therefore unjustified."

Item: On October 7, 1992, Jerry Haaf, a 30-year veteran of the Minneapolis police department assigned to traffic duty, stopped at a pizza shop at 2 A.M. for a cup of coffee. While he was sitting at a table filling out reports, two young black males, in full view of several witnesses, walked up behind him and shot him through the heart. Despite an episode like this, and despite a general rise in crime and gang violence, Minneapolis's liberal city administration continues to insist that police behavior is the city's major problem. Says Mayor Donald Fraser: "I've never met a black family in Minneapolis that hadn't been abused by the police."

It is first necessary to realize that the vast majority of complaints do not involve serious charges.

Item: On September 16, 1992, three off-duty New York City police officers became embroiled in an argument with 18-year-old Ywanus Mohamed as they were entering a subway station. During the argument, Mohamed pulled a box-cutting razor knife and slashed officer John Coughlin in the face, cutting him so badly he nearly died. The wounds required 500 stitches. Officers Thomas Cea and Patrick O'Neill subdued Mohamed, but after they had him handcuffed they allegedly continued punching him and broke his jaw. Mohamed, and Officers Cea and O'Neill, have all equally been charged with felony assault.

Item: Again in New York City, a riot erupted and the entire city spent the summer of 1992 on edge after an undercover police officer named Michael O'Keefe killed 23-year-old Kiko Garcia, a suspected drug dealer, in a street confrontation in Washington Heights. A grand jury eventually exonerated the officer, but Mayor David Dinkins used the occasion to push for the removal of the remaining six police officials from the city's twelve-member police-review board, and to turn it into a completely civilian body.

Item: And again in Brooklyn, on August 19, 1991, in the Crown Heights section, a young Orthodox Jew named Yankel Rosenbaum was set upon by a mob of black teenagers yelling, "Get the Jew." One of them stabbed him, and before he died he identified his killer as Lemrick Nelson, Jr. The police also found a knife in Nelson's possession with blood stains on it that matched Rosenbaum's, and two detectives testified that Nelson had confessed. But on October 30, 1991, in a verdict that seemed to many a mirror image of the Rodney King case, the jury (made up of six blacks, four Hispanics, and two whites) acquitted Nelson of all charges. Evidently the reason was that the jurors did not believe the testimony of the police officers on the scene and concluded that they had framed Nelson. The *New York Times*, which had scarcely been able to contain its outrage over the white and Hispanic jury that had acquitted the police officers in the Rodney King case, now blamed not the jury but the police department—for the crime of having "lost all credibility with the neighborhoods it serves." For good measure, the *Times* also attacked the policemen's union for having "forfeited public faith" through its "callous arrogance." And the moral it drew from the occasion was that the city needed "a more independent board to review complaints of police misconduct."

The problem with civilian review boards

In advancing the bizarre suggestion that the police rather than the criminals are the real problem confronting us, and that the solution therefore lies in civilian oversight, Mayor Dinkins, District Attorney Hynes, Senator Chambers, Mayor Fraser, the *New York Times*, and the many other politicians and media pundits who agree with them, have a good deal of support from the academic world. For example, according to David Bayley, professor of criminology at SUNY Albany, and the leading American authority on foreign police forces,

> We're way behind the rest of the English-speaking world on this issue. England, Canada, Australia, and New Zealand all have strong systems. The best civilian-review board in North America is in Ontario. Their police department has completely lost sovereignty with respect to internal punishments.

Yet that did not prevent Toronto from erupting in riots in June 1992 when a 22-year-old black youth was shot to death by an undercover police officer. Nor is there any evidence that civilian-review boards do any better in this country in defusing the tensions between minority communities and the police.

Sam Walker, professor of criminology at the University of Nebraska, who specializes in civilian-review boards, has just completed a survey in which he found that 35 of the nation's largest cities now have such boards. Walker argues that they act as an outlet to deflect police–civilian confrontations and prevent violence and frustration from building up within poor and minority communities:

> The experience is that when the procedure for filing complaints is made more open to the public, the number of complaints rises. San Francisco has a very open system and has lots of complaints, while Los Angeles has no complaint procedure and is not even talking about one. San Francisco also didn't have any riots. The Mayor of Omaha recently changed the system so that complaints could be filed at city hall rather than at the police stations. The number of complaints immediately doubled. In my judgment, the number of complaints a city has about police brutality is a reflection of public confidence in the police.

Yet public opinion, led by local anti-police activists, is likely to conclude the opposite. First, the number of complaints filed is seen as evidence that police brutality is "widespread." Second, since only a very small number of complaints ever lead to disciplinary action (just as a very small number of criminal complaints ever lead to jail sentences), the vast number that fall apart or are not resolved will usually be taken as proof that "the system isn't working."

The truth, however, is that most complaints are either frivolous or unjustified. This is borne out by the experience of the old New York City Board, which the Vera Institute for Justice, a nonpartisan organization, found to be prejudiced neither for nor against civilians or police officers.

In 1990, the Board's annual report showed a total of 2,376 complaints for "excessive force," 1,140 for "abuse of authority," 1,618 for "discourtesy," and 420 for "ethnic slurs." Among the 2,376 complaints for excessive force (presumably the most serious charge), injuries were documented in 267 cases. These involved 71 bruises, 92 lacerations requiring stitches, 30 fractures, 22 swellings, and 41 "other." In the 2,286 cases that were pursued, 566 were dropped because the complainant became uncooperative, 234 were dropped because the complainant withdrew the charge, and 1,405 were closed with less than full investigation, usually because the complainants became unavailable. Only 81 cases resulted in a finding against the policeman.

To understand why there is such an overload of frivolous cases, it is first necessary to realize that the vast majority of complaints do not involve serious charges. In 80 percent of the New York cases, the complainant did not even seek punishment or further investigation, but only wanted to confront the officer.

Furthermore, the serious complaints are often the work of criminals who are seeking some leverage in the charges against them. "They file a complaint as soon as they are arrested and hope to use it as a trade-off in bargaining their case," says Robert M. Morgenthau, the district attorney of Manhattan. Drug dealers in particular have become adept at using the complaint system as a bargaining tool. In the 34th precinct (Washington Heights), which led all New York City precincts for homicides in 1991, arresting officers now routinely hand drug suspects the civilian-complaint form as an ironic gesture in "community relations."

When Professor Walker was asked to point to a system that works, he replied:

> That's a question I've been asked a hundred times and I don't know the answer. I was talking to a reporter from the *Detroit News* and he told me that Detroit has a strong civilian-review board and few complaints about police brutality. Maybe the system works there. I'm going to have to go up and see.

Detroit, of course, is a city where, as one columnist wrote recently, "the wheels have fallen off Western civilization."

Brutality and charges of racism

There are people who contend that to downgrade the problem of police brutality is to adopt a white perspective and to manifest insensitivity, or worse, to the black condition. No doubt there is some truth to this charge. After all, as Mayor Fraser points out, law-abiding blacks are more likely to be harassed by cops than are their white counterparts, so that for the former, police misconduct is indeed something to worry about. But a cursory glance at the FBI's Uniform Crime Reports makes it clear why focusing on police misbehavior is so perversely misplaced an emphasis.

Since 1986, the incidence of all crimes per 100,000 population is only up 6 percent, and some property crimes (pocket-pickings, purse-snatchings, and motor-vehicle accessory theft) have actually shown a slight decline. But these small decreases in property crimes have been more than offset by a huge increase in personal and violent crimes.

Thus, the rate of violent crime is up 29 percent overall and 24 percent in per-capita terms. Murder rates are up 23 percent and 18 percent per capita. Robbery rates have risen 33 percent in real terms and 28 percent in per-capita terms. This includes an absolute increase of 50 percent for bank robberies, 38 percent for street robberies, 27 percent for convenience-store robberies, 16 percent for residential robberies, and 11 percent for gas-station robberies. Aggravated assault is also up 28 percent in absolute terms and 23 percent per capita.

Does all this mean that America is becoming a far more violent society? Not entirely. What is unique about this crime wave is that it has been confined almost completely to black juveniles. The lines for "white" and "other" (Hispanic, Oriental, American Indian, etc.) are almost perfectly flat over the same period. But the arrest rate for blacks has gone nearly vertical.

From the time they reach physical maturity until the time they disappear into the netherworld of dereliction and homelessness, these young black men lead lives of stupefying violence.

What is more, violent blacks are getting younger and younger. In an analysis of the Uniform Crime Reports, James Alan Fox, dean of the Northeastern University College of Criminal Justice, found that crime rates were up the steepest for the youngest groups. Arrest rates for murder climbed 121 percent for 17-year-olds, 158 percent for 16-year-olds, and 217 percent for 15-year-olds. Even 12-year-olds were up 100 percent.

This unprecedented crime wave among young blacks has hit the cities hardest. Minneapolis, for example, has 40 percent of Minnesota's crime, even though it has only 8 percent of the state's population. In New York, 85 percent of the state's record 2,200 murders in 1990 were in New York City (less than half the state's population). And within New York City, 70 percent of the murders were concentrated in a few neighborhoods—Washington Heights, Harlem, East Harlem, the South Bronx, East New York, and Bedford Stuyvesant. Brooklyn's 75th precinct (East New York), a drug-infested wasteland with a population of 160,000, had more murders than Buffalo, Rochester, Syracuse, and Albany combined (total population 880,000).

The reasons for the upsurge in inner-city violence are by now familiar. The most obvious is the introduction of crack cocaine, which has transformed drug addiction from a messy, disease-ridden, needle-passing subculture to a cleaner, inhaling-based "mainstream" habit among major portions of the underclass population. Once again, the arrest statistics reflect this change. While juvenile arrests for marijuana and other drugs are down or level since 1985, arrests for cocaine have soared during the same period. And once again, this increase has been concentrated entirely among blacks.

Beyond that, there is the disintegration of normal social life in many black ghettos. What is most striking is the loss of the mediating institutions of society—the churches, stores, schools, voluntary organizations, commercial activities, and ordinary street life that once formed a buffer between criminals and law-abiding citizens. On the streets surrounding the Robert Taylor Homes, a dreaded housing project on the South Side of Chicago, there is little sign of life except for a few graffiti-scarred playgrounds and scattered rows of desolate—though still inhabited—homes. Among the ruined buildings are an abandoned factory and a burned-out YMCA. Over nearly twenty square blocks, the only commercial advertising is a ubiquitous billboard on the back of bus-stop benches, advertising: "Beepers. Call 633-9610." Beepers, of course, are the standard equipment of the drug trade.

Police are out-gunned

Most forbidding of all, however, is the collapse of history's oldest bulwark against crime and violent behavior—the nuclear family.

The majority of black males in ghetto areas no longer have any real adult role to play, either at home or in society. Their role as breadwinner—however poorly it may have been played in the past—has now been usurped by the welfare system. In projects like the Robert Taylor Homes, where more than 90 percent of the households involve only women and children, adult men have all but disappeared.

Over half of all black children born in this country are now born to unwed mothers, and in many poor areas, the figure exceeds 80 percent. Some of these women may supplement their welfare grant with some kind of furtive arrangement with a new man. But family units built around stable marriages are essentially unknown.

Nationwide, 25 percent of black men between the ages of 15 and 35 are entangled in the criminal-justice system—as prison inmates, defendants, parolees, or probationers. In cities like Washington, the number approaches 40 percent. Homicide is now the most common cause of death for black men between the ages of 20 and 35, and 1 in every 22 black men can expect to be murdered.

From the time they reach physical maturity until the time they disappear into the netherworld of dereliction and homelessness, these young black men lead lives of stupefying violence. In this unrelenting free-for-all, there are no qualms about killing someone for a pair of sneakers or sunglasses or because the other person is wearing the wrong colors or looks the wrong way. Listen to the voices of Sidewinder and Bopete, two 14-year-olds, as recorded in a California youth-detention center by Léon Bing for her chronicle of Los Angeles gang life, *Do or Die:*

> [Bopete:] "Sometimes I think about not goin' back to bangin' when I get outta here. I play in sports a lot here, and I. . . ."
>
> Sidewinder's laugh interrupts. "Sound like a regular ol' teenager, don't he? I sound like that, too, after the drive-by. I got shot twice in the leg, 'cause they was shootin' at the car, and when that happen I didn't want to bang no more, either. Makin' promises to God, all like that. But when it heal up. . . ." He is silent for a moment; maybe he's thinking about a freedom he won't taste for a while. Then, "I tell you somethin'—I don't feel connected to any other kids in this city or in this country or in this world. I only feel com-

fortable in my 'hood. That's the only thing I'm connected to, that's my family. One big family—that's about it."

"In my 'hood, in the Jungle, it ain't like a gang. It's more like a nation, everybody all together as one. Other kids, as long as they ain't my enemies, I can be cool with 'em." Bopete lapses into silence. "I'll tell you, though—if I didn't have no worst enemy to fight with, I'd probably find somebody."

"Ye-eeeeeeh," Sidewinder picks it up. "*I'd* find somebody. 'Cause if they ain't nobody to fight, it ain't no gangs. It ain't no life. I don't know . . . it ain't no. . . ."

"It ain't no fun."

"Yeah! Ain't no fun just sittin' there. Anybody can just sit around, just drink, smoke a little Thai. But that ain't fun like shootin' guns and stabbin' people. *That's* fun."

It might seem that nothing more could be piled atop this disintegrating social scene to make a policeman's life more difficult and dangerous. But something has been: the proliferation of illegal guns, particularly automatic and semi-automatic weapons.

Says Hubert Williams, head of the Police Foundation:

There's a strong feeling among the departments around the country that we're being outgunned in our own neighborhoods. You can see it in the number of high-power, high-tech weapons confiscated off the streets. I mean, add it up. There are only about 70 patrolmen in every precinct and each one has one gun. How many guns are there in the neighborhoods we're patrolling?

The speed and sophistication of the weapons in the hands of today's drug dealers have made the rap singer Ice Cube's description of South Central Los Angeles—"the concrete Vietnam"—no exaggeration. According to Jack Killorin, of the Federal Bureau of Alcohol, Tobacco, and Firearms:

The kind of semi-automatic weapons in the hands of criminals today means even one bad guy can do a devastating amount of damage. It's not necessarily the power of the guns—although certainly that makes a difference. But many criminals are now armed with semi-automatic weapons that can literally fill the air with bullets. Not only are guns faster and more powerful, but there's an almost psychopathic willingness to use them.

In 1981, American gunmakers manufactured 1.7 million revolvers and 837,000 semi-automatic pistols. In 1991, the ratio was completely reversed—1.3 million semi-automatics to 456,000 revolvers. Standard revolvers, carried by most police officers, fire six shots and then require reloading, while semi-automatic pistols usually contain a clip of 16–24 bullets. "It's during that reloading time, when the first round of bullets runs out, that a lot of officers are killed," says Killorin.

Nevertheless, in New York City, Mayor Dinkins—against the urging of the FBI—personally prevented the police from switching to semi-automatic 9-mm. weapons, even though such weapons were carried by his own bodyguards.

Order maintenance and community policing

What can we expect the police to do under these circumstances?

In 1968, James Q. Wilson examined the problem in his classic book,

Varieties of Police Behavior. In that long-lost era, when the principal problems of police work involved dealing with drunks and breaking up fights at parties, Wilson discovered three styles of police action, which he termed the "watchman," the "legalistic," and the "service."

The "watchman," or "order-maintenance" style, common in cities with old political machines, tended to concentrate on maintaining order, giving individual patrolmen a lot of latitude to enforce the law as they saw fit. Large concentrations of gambling and prostitution were usually tolerated—often in black neighborhoods—as long as they did not offend the "respectable" people of the town.

The truth is, in the current climate, a cop is more worried about getting in trouble than getting killed.

The "legalistic" departments had usually been through some kind of reform period. Police stuck by the letter of the law and were impeccable about corruption. They wrote speeding tickets on an equal basis for city councilmen and black ghetto residents alike. The police force had usually been put out of the reach of politics and a strict civil-service or merit system prevailed.

The "service" style was a kind of middle ground, found mostly in the suburbs. The police were not "pro-active," but extremely conscious of the desires of their constituents. The law was upheld in a neutral way, but the police were unobtrusive about it as well. Although this style worked well in homogeneous suburbs, Wilson doubted that it could serve as a model in heterogeneous urban populations.

Regrettably enough, Wilson discovered that both the laissez-faire order-maintenance style *and* the reform-minded legalistic style (which was in many ways its opposite) *both* aroused resentment in black communities:

> Order maintenance means managing conflict, and conflict implies disagreeing over what should be done, how, and to whom. Conflict is found in all social strata and thus in all strata there will be resentment, often justified, against particular police interventions (or their absence), but in lower-class areas conflict and disorder will be especially common and thus such resentment will be especially keen. It is hardly surprising that polls show young lower-income Negro males as being deeply distrustful of and bitter about the police; it would be a mistake, however, to assume that race is the decisive factor.

But when minimal order-maintenance (which had been the rule in the South) gave way to a stricter effort to impose middle-class standards on the entire community, the resentment remained. In Wilson's words:

> One reason for the increasing complaints of "police harassment" may be that, in the large cities, Negroes are being brought under a single standard of justice; one reason for the complaints of discrimination may be that this process is proceeding unevenly and imperfectly. As the populations of our large cities become, through continued migration, more heavily Negro, more heavily lower-income, and more youthful, we can expect these complaints to increase in number and frequency, especially if, as seems likely, organizations competing for leadership in the central cities continue to seek out such issues in order to attract followers.

Having so accurately foreseen what was coming, Wilson (in collaboration with George Kelling) later developed the well-known "broken-windows" hypothesis, which has served as the basis of the "neighborhood-policing" movement. Wilson and Kelling decided that the watchman style had been correct in one respect—order-maintenance does matter. "A broken window that remains broken is a signal that no one cares and an invitation for more broken windows," they wrote. Or, as a resident of Washington Heights put it during the tensions in the summer of 1992:

> I know the police are never going to clean up the drug problem in this neighborhood because they can't even deal with the problem of double-parked cars.

Wilson and Kelling's neighborhood policing is now the basis of a reform movement that is being instituted all over the country—even in places where it does not seem entirely appropriate. Foot patrolmen are now walking the beats of South-Central Los Angeles, trying to win the trust of the community—even though in such neighborhoods they may be the only people around not traveling by car.

Police brutality is not the problem

But whether or not neighborhood policing will do any good, one thing remains clear: to concentrate on police "harassment" and "brutality" is to divert attention from the real problem that faces our society, which is the terrible upsurge of violent crime since 1988. Worse yet, this focus creates a climate and leads to policies which can only have the effect of making it harder for the police to do their job, and perhaps also of making them less willing to do it.

In Los Angeles in May 1992, the police department hesitated to mount a show of force when the Rodney King verdict was handed down because officials feared they would be blamed for igniting violence. "It would have been seen as provocative," said Willie Williams, who succeeded Daryl Gates as L.A. police chief in June 1992. As it was, there were many reports of police passivity in the face of looting and arson, and order was not restored until three days later when 9,000 National Guardsmen and federal troops hit the streets.

In Minneapolis (which not only has a civilian-review board but also an organization in which members of the major drug gangs work together with the police in trying to establish domestic tranquility), the cops are feeling anxious and inhibited. Says Jerry Larson, a veteran detective and vice president of the city's Police Federation (the policemen's union):

> The mayor told us for years that gangs here wouldn't be a problem. We warned him they would and now we've got a problem. You can't handle these gangs without getting pro-active, and having all this constant criticism from the political establishment makes us real leery about doing our jobs. It'll be like New York, where the police just drive by things. I know some New York coppers and they say, "The hell with it. If those people aren't killing each other, we're not getting out of our cars."

In New York City itself, as though to confirm Larson's observation, Officer Todd Jamison declared in responding to charges of police brutality after an arrest that left one of his colleagues injured: "There are certain things where we have the power of discretion, we can turn our heads and say, why get involved?" An even more striking comment was made by Officer O'Keefe. When asked why he had not drawn his gun sooner in his mortal struggle with Garcia in Washington Heights, O'Keefe replied: "The truth is, in the current climate, a cop is more worried about getting in trouble than getting killed."

A poignant incident that occurred in Chicago drives the point home. When the Chicago Bulls won the National Basketball Association championship in June 1992, thousands of the city's residents—nearly all of them black—celebrated by rampaging through the downtown stores, breaking windows, looting, and turning over parked cars. (The *New York Times* reported that, of the 100 people injured during the riots, 94 were police officers.) Picking up a pattern which had been established in the Los Angeles riot a month before, the mobs singled out Korean-owned businesses for attack. Park Jung, the 32-year-old owner of a men's clothing store on the West Side, found more than 100 people trying to break through his storefront. When he appealed for help to several police officers who were standing idly by, they refused, advising him to "take care of your life and go home." He left and his store was destroyed.

"What else could I do?" Mr. Park said. "I hate America. I'm going back to Korea."

But those of us who are staying here in America will have greater and greater cause to rue the fact that the police are being morally disarmed and demoralized by a climate of opinion that seems to regard them as a bigger threat to society than the criminals they have to confront—and by whom they are being increasingly outgunned. For many years, criminologists have tried to dismiss swings in the crime rate with the bland assertion that they represent shifts in the crime-prone population of young males. But the current outburst has occurred during a trough in the population cycle. As Dean Fox points out:

> What we've seen in the past few years is nothing compared with what we'll see in the next decade and on into the next century. Right now, we have the fewest 18-to-24-year-olds we've had since 1965, but next year they will start to go back up.

In other words, the worst is yet to come, and if the police continue to be incapacitated by a fixation on their occasional misbehavior, we—and most especially the young blacks among us—will have even less protection against violent crime in the future than we do today.

8

Police Brutality Is Not a Widespread Problem

Lawrence B. Sulc

Lawrence B. Sulc is president of the Nathan Hale Foundation in Washington, D.C., and is a regular contributor to Conservative Review.

Police are a "thin blue line" between society and criminals, and they should be supported in the fight against crime. Television news and entertainment shows, as well as some politicians, often portray police officers as brutal, when in fact brutality complaints have declined. The stresses of the job—facing criminals every day, a revolving-door criminal justice system, hostile media—sometimes cause police to use excessive force, but assaults on police officers far outnumber complaints of police misconduct. Police brutality is a serious matter and officers should be severely punished when it occurs, but it is not the biggest problem facing the nation—crime is. To prevent police brutality, police officers should be given respect and support by citizens and counseling through employee assistance programs.

The "thin blue line" is up against it. In most of the country the police continue to command public trust and respect but without doubt in some areas, especially in the larger cities, there is a serious problem of confidence. The news media, as is to be expected, make the most of it. Turmoil is more newsworthy than order and consternation is more interesting than easy sailing. To a large degree the media, both the news and the entertainment sides—if they can be so divided—actually contribute to the agitation; ". . . current images of the police are drawn largely from television programs bearing little resemblance to reality," charges Edwin J. Delattre in his bench-mark work, *Character and Cops: Ethics in Policing.*[1] TV helps create the warped image of the police in America today.

There are, moreover, special interest groups and individuals whose reason for being is conflict with authority. Who "represents authority more than the police?" Many of these dissidents keep the pot boiling, as it were, while skimming off the seemingly limitless financial support from Hollywood. Then there are the politicians whose cleavage to fiery local pressure groups wins them reelection. "The real money to be made

Lawrence B. Sulc, "The Children of Chaos and the Thin Blue Line," *Conservative Review*, October 1992. Reprinted with permission.

on racial and poverty issues is to be made on the political left," says Thomas Sowell, conservative columnist.[2] Sowell might well have included "police bashing," as well, the three issues often being intertwined.

Complaints of police brutality

There is no excuse for wanton police violence. It simply cannot be justified in any society. The Los Angeles incident [the Rodney King arrest] has "made everyone's job in law enforcement more difficult and dangerous," according to the editors of *Police Times*.[3]

Judge William Sessions, director of the FBI, told the National Association for the Advancement of Colored People not long ago that 50 percent of all FBI civil rights investigations involve complaints of police brutality.[4] Cops sometimes use unnecessary force.

Yes, cops sometimes use unnecessary force. They also use extraordinary restraint. On countless occasions every day, in dealing with the burgeoning wave of violence that is almost overwhelming them, police officers refrain from exercising the force that they could easily get away with. Understandably, no statistics are available for this category.

"In fact, police brutality may actually be less prevalent today than it was twenty years ago," says the news magazine *New Dimensions*. "Civil liberties groups and police departments report fewer brutality complaints filed in recent years, not more," the magazine points out. "And while the FBI's Civil Rights Division reports 2,450 complaints involving law enforcement in 1989, during the same period, 62,172 law enforcement officers were victims of assaults."[5] In 1990, there were more than 71,794 assaults against law enforcement officers nationwide, according to the FBI's *Uniform Crime Reports*. Sixty-five officers were killed. Sixty-seven more lost their lives as a result of accidents in connection with the performance of their official duties. Total: 132. Veterans of military combat among the police say that street violence around the country today reminds them of Vietnam, reports *The Badge*.[6]

Police officers put their lives on the line every time they put on their uniforms. Frequently forced to make split-second, life-or-death decisions, they really never know when such instances will arise. Their antagonists on the streets and in the alleys are often unpredictable or, if predictable, predictably bad. At best, cops aren't always dealing with the better elements of society but, as Dorothy Uhnak, a former detective, calls them in her book, *Policewoman*, ". . . the vilest and the lowest and most depraved forms of humanity. . .".[7]

Beset almost constantly with trouble, frequently serious, sometimes deadly, the police are sorely tested. Often. Daily. It is the nature of the business. For many it is war—what G.K. Chesterton had in mind when he wrote, "By dealing with the unsleeping sentinels who guard the outposts of society, it tends to remind us that we live in an armed camp, making war with a chaotic world, and that the criminals, the children of chaos, are nothing but traitors within our gates. . . ."[8]

Handling constant stress

With combat goes stress. Because of the special nature of their jobs, "(p)olice officers die younger, suffer more injuries and stress-related disabilities than the average American," according to Officer Gary Hankins, chairman of the labor committee of the Fraternal Order of Police [FOP] in

Washington, D.C. "We have high rates of alcoholism, divorce and suicide," he told *The Washington Post.*[9]

The problems are not just a matter of "traditional" stress, however, Hankins told me, but the frustration stemming from a lack of support from the system.[10] Officers, however altruistic their motives in the beginning of their careers, are placed in "a system doomed to fail," he claims. Their sense of justice is battered and their initiative stifled when the 40,000 felons arrested annually in the District of Columbia are forced into a judicial system that can actually try only 750. "Politicians want to erode their retirement, prosecutors want to drop their cases and judges want to release their prisoners," Hankins said. Police officers are dismayed and disheartened with telling effect.

As police everywhere point out, they make plenty of arrests. Of every 100 of their hard-won felony arrests, however, according to *U.S. News & World Report*, 43 defendants "walk." They are not prosecuted and their cases are dismissed. Plea bargains account for 53 of the remaining 57 cases. Two of the three defendants who actually make it to court are found guilty. A friend of mine was once robbed at gun point. His courageous response led to the arrest of the robber but, upon leaving the police station after being questioned, he was unnerved to spot the gunman eyeing him intently from across the street. The *crook* was out before *he* was. The curious thing about this case is that the felon actually did time. The victim risked his life to give chase and help bring the perpetrator to justice, it should be noted. The police and the K9 auxiliary, on the other hand, were exemplary—that is, after the latter was persuaded not to bite the victim of the robbery but go for the gunman, instead.

Beset almost constantly with trouble, frequently serious, sometimes deadly, the police are sorely tested. Often. Daily.

The trouble is that prosecutors can't pursue convictions and judges can't sentence if there isn't enough prison space. Although beefing up prosecutorial staffs and building more cells is expensive, it is actually cost effective. Increasingly, studies show that it is much less expensive to imprison convicted felons and hold them longer than to unloose them on society to continue their depredations. Eugene Methvin, a senior editor of *Reader's Digest*, revealed data on the tremendous costs to society of the early release of prisoners and the benefits of keeping them in.[11] William Rusher, the columnist, cites the work of James Austin of the National Council on Crime and Delinquency and the research of David Cavanaugh and Mark Kleiman of Harvard in support of this point.[12]

Our elected public officials must do better by the police. I always thought, and still do, that assault on a police officer was a serious crime. Yet, watching live TV coverage of hooligans and looters stoning and firebombing the police in the Spring 1991 Mt. Pleasant Avenue riots in Washington, D.C., without an immediate, forceful and adequate response from the police, was infuriating. Fortunately, I was not among the assaulted. Nonetheless, I cannot help but wonder how the victims—the police—felt under such bombardment while restrained by orders from above.

The police were ill-equipped and poorly led during those disorders.

The Metropolitan Police Department [MPD] has no management training program, according to Officer Hankins[13] and so it seemed in watching its poor handling of the Mt. Pleasant Avenue riots. A casual observer might be excused if he thought the District showed more concern for the rioters than for the owners of the stores being looted, while the police on the line stood by, taking hits, unable to respond adequately.

When the Immigration and Naturalization Service arrived to identify and perhaps move to deport the illegal aliens among the apprehended rioters, the city administration refused cooperation. No telling what might happen if the law (in this case federal immigration law) were enforced and certain criminals (arrested rioters who were also in the country illegally) were deported. Seemingly, everyone would benefit in such cases— except the criminals, of course—and perhaps that was the point.

In sum, let the police do their job. If they violate the law, come down hard on them as the criminals they are when they break the law they have sworn to uphold. There are a few bad cops and they must be rooted out.

Loyalty and the code of silence

A major barrier to effective police self-policing, however, is the unwillingness of many officers to report the wrongdoing of others, especially their partners. Such loyalty, while understandable, is misplaced. Loyalty is properly given to the department and the community and most especially the law, the law being the "reason for being" of the police. The "code of silence" is more appropriate to the mafia than to the police. "Courageous persons will not tolerate . . . abuses," says Delattre, in writing of that essential loyalty between partners in police work. "A [police] colleague who deserves to be a friend . . . would not compromise a partner," he says. "The betrayal of office is an affront to honesty and justice as well as friendship."[14]

"Living up to the public trust is demanding work," Delattre acknowledges. "It can involve disappointment, weariness and stress. These are the facts of life in police work. But this is the work that each police officer has chosen for himself."[15]

Police officers have accepted high standards. They should be held to those standards. Other public officials who have command, supervisory and review functions over them should be held to standards equally high. Their lives, after all, are not in such grave danger so much of the time as are those of line police officers. They should support the departments and the men and women in them.

Of every 100 of their hard-won felony arrests, . . . 43 defendants "walk.". . . Plea bargains account for 53 of the remaining 57 cases.

Citizens should be held to standards, too. All should understand the unusual problems both officers and departments face. Among other things, citizens should encourage and support community police counseling programs like the Metropolitan Police Employee Assistance Program (MPEAP) in Washington, D.C., a joint management/labor effort conducted by the FOP on behalf of the MPD. Confidentiality, essential to such programs, is ensured by the separation of the EAP from departmental management. The MPEAP staff consists of police officers as well as contract civilian counselors, combining the special contributions of each profession.

Employee counseling programs, helping police deal with their numerous serious problems, exist in many but not all departments. Interestingly, the MPEAP in Washington is managed by another Officer Hankins—Mrs. Janet Hankins, wife of Officer Gary Hankins, mentioned above—who says the MPEAP gets hundreds of new clients every year. She too, of course, refers to the stress in police work with which she is familiar from her many years as a police officer.

Tougher law enforcement is needed

Police violence, although unquestionably a matter of serious import, is not as bad as it appears. It is exacerbated by warped media treatment both in fiction (network shows) and in reporting (network news). The unusual stress of police work contributes to the overreaction of cops—the overreaction of media and public to the cops contribute to the stress. Everyone who cares about these issues—and everyone should—should pause to reflect. At the root of the problems are the criminals. In much of the country the judicial system, unable to cope with the numbers of apprehended criminals, returns them to the streets. They are not nice people. Many are downright evil. Officer Janet Hankins has seen police officers traumatized after having to shoot someone in the line of duty while many crooks are not traumatized at the taking of a life, she observes.

The nation needs tougher law enforcement, fewer plea bargains and more time served of the sentences that are handed down. To achieve these ends, more cells are needed to keep the convicted felons in. Of course, solving the problems that contribute to crime is essential and must be addressed, but failure to face these immediate needs immediately is producing disaster.

Police violence, although unquestionably a matter of serious import, is not as bad as it appears.

Officer Hankins has her own recommendations. Both the criminals and the police work 24 hours a day, she pointed out. Communities should demand night "papering" and night courts to process the arrests that are flooding the system. More convicted felons should be imprisoned for long periods both for deterrence and for punishment, she said. And to keep them off the street.

To help, citizens can join neighborhood watch programs and cooperate with the police, according to Officer Janet Hankins. They should never intervene at the scene of an incident, as is often the case, she warned. An officer at such time is under great pressure and is likely to feel personally threatened by interference. A lot of officers are hurt in situations like this. If necessary, the citizen should go to the police station to sign on as a witness or to register a complaint.

Citizens can help by treating the police with whom they come in contact with more respect, Officer Hankins pointed out. "They should be more polite," she said simply, always aware of the stress of the occasion. Of course such courtesy should be matched by the police, she agrees.

If the system were to actually break down, we would call out the National Guard and/or jury rig a regime of vigilantes but, in due time, finding such a system less than satisfactory, we would respond to the need for a highly motivated, well-trained and equipped, competently led police force. We must, of course, prevent the breakdown and work for those goals now with what we have in place.

In the meanwhile, the police need and deserve public support—they are our "thin blue line" locked in a warlike struggle with Chesterton's "children of chaos." Behind that "thin blue line" is where we stand, with our loved ones.

On the other hand, if things go from bad to worse, maybe we can get off by pleading insanity.

Notes

1. *Character and Cops: Ethics in Policing*, Edwin J. Delattre, American Enterprise Institute of Public Policy Research, Washington, D.C., 1989, p. 29.

2. *The Washington Times*, July 29, 1991, D3.

3. *Police Times*, American Federation of Police, May/June 1991, p. 4.

4. *The Washington Post*, June 7, 1991, A16.

5. *New Dimensions*, August, 1991, p. 18.

6. *The Badge*, July 1991, p. 5.

7. As quoted by Delattre, ibid, p. 157.

8. As quoted by Delattre, ibid, p. v.i.

9. *The Washington Post*, July 27, 1991.

10. Telephone interview, July 30, 1991.

11. *Reader's Digest*, June 1991.

12. W.A. Rusher, *Human Events*, Aug. 3, 1991, p. 13.

13. Telephone interview, op cit.

14. Delattre, *Ibid*, p. 11.

15. Delattre, *Ibid*, p. 33.

Organizations to Contact

The editors have compiled the following list of organizations concerned with the issues debated in this book. The descriptions are derived from materials provided by the organizations. All have publications or information available for interested readers. The list was compiled on the date of publication of the present volume; names, addresses, and phone numbers may change. Be aware that many organizations take several weeks or longer to respond to inquiries, so allow as much time as possible.

American Civil Liberties Union (ACLU)
132 W. 43rd St.
New York, NY 10036
(212) 944-9800

The ACLU is a national organization that works to defend Americans' civil rights guaranteed in the U.S. Constitution. Among other services, the ACLU provides legal assistance to victims of police abuse. The ACLU publishes and distributes the manual *Fighting Police Abuse: A Community Action Manual*.

The Heritage Foundation
214 Massachusetts Ave. NE
Washington, DC 20002
(202) 546-4400

The foundation is a public policy research institute dedicated to the principles of free enterprise and limited government. It publishes occasional papers on current public policy issues in its periodic *Backgrounder*, among them "An Empowerment Strategy for Eliminating Neighborhood Crime," which outlines a community policing program.

International Association of Chiefs of Police (IACP)
515 N. Washington St.
Alexandria, VA 22314
(703) 836-6767

The association consists of police executives who provide consultation and research services to, and support educational programs for, police departments nationwide. The association publishes *Police Chief* magazine monthly, which covers all aspects of law enforcement duty.

National Association for the Advancement of Colored People (NAACP)
4805 Mt. Hope Dr.
Baltimore, MD 21215
(301) 481-4100

The NAACP is a civil rights organization that focuses particularly on ending racial discrimination in America. It researches and documents police brutality and provides legal services for victims of brutality. The NAACP publishes the magazine *Crisis* ten times per year.

National Coalition on Police Accountability (NCOPA)
Citizens Alert
59 E. Van Buren, Suite 2418
Chicago, IL 60605
(312) 663-5392

The coalition consists of community, legal, and law enforcement groups working to hold police accountable to their communities through legislation, litigation, community organizing, and civilian oversight. NCOPA provides referral to community review organizations nationwide. Citizens Alert is Chicago's community review organization and a clearinghouse for NCOPA information.

National Institute of Justice (NIJ)
National Criminal Justice Reference Service (NCJRS)
Box 6000
Rockville, MD 20850
(301) 251-5500
(800) 851-3420

A component of the Office of Justice Programs of the U.S. Department of Justice, the NIJ supports and conducts research on crime, criminal behavior, and crime prevention. The NCJRS acts as a clearinghouse for criminal justice information for researchers and other interested individuals. It publishes and distributes reports and books, including reports of the Bureau of Justice Statistics.

Police Executive Research Forum (PERF)
1100 Connecticut Ave. NW, Suite 930
Washington, DC 20036
(202) 466-7820

PERF is a national professional association of police executives that seeks to increase public understanding and stimulate debate on important criminal justice issues. PERF publishes numerous books, occasional papers, and periodicals, including *Police Agency Handling of Citizen Complaints: A Model Policy Statement* and *Problem-Oriented Policing.*

Police Foundation
1001 22nd St. NW, Suite 200
Washington, DC 20037
(202) 833-1460

The foundation conducts research projects on police practices and aims to improve the quality of police personnel. It publishes the book *Police Use of Force: Official Reports, Citizen Complaints, and Legal Consequences* and distributes *The City in Crisis: A Report by the Special Advisor to the Board of Police Commissioners on the Civil Disorder in Los Angeles.*

Bibliography

Books

Edwin J. Delattre	*Character and Cops: Ethics in Policing.* Washington: American Enterprise Institute, 1989.
Audrey Farrell	*Crime, Class and Corruption: The Politics of the Police.* Chicago: Bookmarks, 1992.
Daryl F. Gates with Diane K. Shah	*Chief: My Life in the LAPD.* New York: Bantam Books, 1992.
Herman Goldstein	*Problem-Oriented Policing.* Philadelphia: Temple University Press, 1990.
George L. Kelling and William J. Bratton	*Implementing Community Policing: The Administrative Problem.* Perspectives on Policing series, no. 17. Washington: U.S. Dept. of Justice, 1993.
George L. Kelling and Mark H. Moore	*The Evolving Strategy of Policing.* Perspectives on Policing series, no. 4. Washington: U.S. Dept. of Justice, 1989.
Knapp Commission	*The Knapp Commission Report on Police Corruption.* Commission to Investigate Allegations of Police Corruption and the City's Anti-Corruption Procedures. New York: George Braziller, 1972.
Stacey C. Koon with Robert Deitz	*Presumed Guilty: The Tragedy of the Rodney King Affair.* Washington: Regnery Gateway, 1992.
Susan Ehrlich Martin	*On the Move: The Status of Women in Policing.* Washington: Police Foundation, 1990. Available from 1001 22nd St. NW, Suite 200, Washington, DC 20037.
Edwin Meese III	*Community Policing and the Police Officer.* Perspectives on Policing series, no. 15. Washington: U.S. Dept. of Justice, 1993.
Wesley G. Skogan	*Disorder and Decline: Crime and the Spiral of Decay in American Neighborhoods.* New York: Free Press, 1990.
Malcolm K. Sparrow, Mark H. Moore, and David M. Kennedy	*Beyond 911: A New Era for Policing.* New York: Basic Books, 1990.
William Spelman and John E. Eck	*Problem-Oriented Policing.* Research in Brief series. Washington: U.S. Dept. of Justice, 1987.
Michael Tonry and Norval Morris, eds.	*Modern Policing.* Chicago: University of Chicago Press, 1992.
Robert C. Trojanowicz and B. Bucqueroux	*Community Policing.* Cincinnati: Anderson Publishing Co., 1990.
William Tucker	*Vigilante: The Backlash Against Crime in America.* New York: Stein and Day, 1985.
Robert Wasserman and Mark H. Moore	*Values in Policing.* Perspectives on Policing series, no. 8. Washington: U.S. Dept. of Justice, 1989.

Hubert Williams and Patrick V. Murphy — *The Evolving Strategy of Police: A Minority View.* Perspectives on Policing series, no. 13. Washington: U.S. Dept. of Justice, 1990.

Periodicals

Nicolas Alexander — "Taming the Paramilitary Monster," *Third Force*, September/October 1993.

Lee P. Brown — "Community Policing: Bring the Community into the Battle Against Crime," *Vital Speeches of the Day*, July 1, 1992.

Tucker Carlson — "D.C. Blues," *Policy Review*, Winter 1993.

Sarah Chayes — "Black Faces, Black Masks," *Reconstruction*, vol. 2, no. 1, 1992. Available from 1563 Massachusetts Ave., Cambridge, MA 02138.

Reuben M. Greenberg — "Less Bang-Bang for the Buck," *Policy Review*, Winter 1992.

Carl F. Horowitz — "An Empowerment Strategy for Eliminating Neighborhood Crime," The Heritage Foundation *Backgrounder*, March 5, 1991. Available from 214 Massachusetts Ave. NE, Washington, DC 20002-4999.

Jon Katz — "Cop Killers? The Media Target the Police," *Rolling Stone*, January 21, 1993.

Vicki Kemper — "Biting the Bullet," *Common Cause Magazine*, Winter 1992.

Tracey Maclin — "Black and Blue: African-Americans and the Police," *Reconstruction*, vol. 2, no. 1, 1992.

Edwin Meese III and Bob Carrico — "Taking Back the Streets: Police Methods That Work," *Policy Review*, Fall 1990.

Dirk Roggeveen — "Better Fed Than Dead: Why Make Police Brutality a Federal Case," *Reason*, August/September 1992.

Jennifer Vogel — "The Pro-Police Review Board," *The Nation*, January 6, 1992.

Gordon Witkin — "What the LAPD Ought to Try," *U.S. News & World Report*, May 11, 1992.

Index